# Sell Your Nonfiction Book

## Crawford Kilian

**Self-Counsel Press**
*(a division of)*
International Self-Counsel Press Ltd.
USA    Canada

*Self-Counsel Press acknowledges the financial support of the Government of Canada through the Book Publishing Industry Development Program (BPIDP) for our publishing activities.*

*Printed in Canada.*

*First edition: 2009*


**Library and Archives Canada Cataloguing in Publication**

Kilian, Crawford, 1941-

    Sell your nonfiction book / Crawford Kilian.

ISBN 978-1-55180-853-6

    1. Authorship--Marketing.  2. Authorship.  I. Title.

PN145.K52 2009         808'.02         C2009-902331-8

**Mixed Sources**
Cert no. SW-COC-001271
© 1996 FSC

FSC

**Self-Counsel Press**
(*a division of*)
International Self-Counsel Press Ltd.

1481 Charlotte Road      1704 North State Street
North Vancouver, BC  V7J 1H1      Bellingham, WA  98225
Canada                    USA

# Contents

# Notice to Readers

Laws are constantly changing. Every effort is made to keep this publication as current as possible. However, the author, the publisher, and the vendor of this book make no representations or warranties regarding the outcome or the use to which the information in this book is put and are not assuming any liability for any claims, losses, or damages arising out of the use of this book. The reader should not rely on the author or publisher of this book for any professional advice. Please be sure that you have the most recent edition.

# Introduction

Writing nonfiction books is fun. I've published six of them, three in multiple editions.

But I couldn't make a living at it; hardly anyone can.

The arithmetic is just about impossible. Suppose you could write 2,000 words a day of finished, publishable nonfiction — about eight double-spaced pages of manuscript. Writing for 30 days without a break, you could complete a 60,000-word regional history or family memoir.

For that book, if it's your first and you're not a famous person, you might expect an advance of perhaps $5,000 (or much, much less) from an American publisher. A Canadian hardcover publisher would pay perhaps half that. In both countries, some publishers pay no advance at all.

But even if you did get an advance, you wouldn't get your money at the end of the month. You'd get it months after your publisher accepted the manuscript (which would be months after you submitted it). You'd get it in installments — probably a third on signing the contract, a third on acceptance of the revised manuscript, and a third on publication.

If the book sold extremely well, you might see more money in a year or two. Otherwise, the advance would be it.

Well, suppose you launch straight into your next book, finish it in a month, and sell it also. And keep doing it every month, for years.

Some writers do just that. After a few years, if they attract enough readers, they will indeed start bringing in enough income every month to allow them to write full-time. Their advances may increase dramatically, perhaps to $25,000 a book or even more. Then they can afford to slow down and take more time.

Only a tiny fraction of published authors succeed this way. And if they don't enjoy what they write, they're no better off than when they made a living flipping hamburgers.

In any case, most publishers don't want to bring out a title a month from a single author, so you'd have to publish under pen names, or deal with several publishers, or both. You'd spend as much time keeping track of your contracts as you'd spend writing.

You could also make a case that full-time writing can isolate an author from the stimulus of the world of ordinary work; pretty soon you might be able to write only about the sufferings of the full-time writer.

Even if you're fated to become a fabulously wealthy author someday, right now you've got to pay the rent and buy the groceries. So you've got a day job. You probably have friends, a spouse or partner, kids, a social life, a dental appointment. They all make demands on your time. If you take three months off, lock yourself in your study, and bash away at your book, your friends and family pay a certain price whether they want to or not.

I know exactly the predicament you're in, because I've been in it all my writing life. For 40 years I held a full-time day job as a college instructor, and I also write and edit for an online magazine. My wife and I share the housework, we raised our kids together, and we've dealt with all the usual crises and demands on our time. Whether I find inspiration or not, the dogs need a walk and the grass needs mowing.

Nevertheless, this is my 21st published book since 1968, including 6 nonfiction books, 3 textbooks, a children's book, and 11 novels — plus over 600 articles. I've done it by writing a little bit for a short time almost every day. It adds up with surprising speed.

Better said, it adds up if you don't make time-consuming mistakes. You can write 5,000 words a day and be no further ahead if you look at it the next morning and decide to scrap it all as hopeless. If you take a couple of years to write an unpublishable book, you're not really better off than the day you started.

The key to successful writing for the novice is to reduce wasted effort to a minimum by *doing things right the first time*.

A simple example: You write a pretty fair self-help or technical book, but it's in the form of a single-spaced manuscript full of grammatical errors and bad punctuation. The editors who see this manuscript will rightly decide that you have passed on too much work to them. They have plenty of other equally good submissions to choose from, by writers who've bothered to proofread and format their manuscripts properly. So why should they spend extra time cleaning up your mess?

A less obvious example: You write a highly literate popular-science book and send it to a string of prestigious publishers. But they don't publish popular science, don't know the market, and aren't about to plunge into it with an unknown author like you. Your book gets nowhere.

An all-too-obvious example: You decide to write a memoir about your amazing family; you write 20 pages, and bog down. Three weeks later you go back, rewrite the 20 pages, and bog down again. And so it goes for months or years.

A twenty-first century example: You have a great idea for a book but it requires a lot of research — into your family history, or your unit's experience in Afghanistan, or how people cope with Lou Gehrig's Disease. You have no idea how to find that information. Worse yet, you hear that book publishers are in big economic trouble and won't consider anything but a "blockbuster" book.

If you know what you're doing, and you plan properly, you can write a book in an hour or two a day, including highly efficient online research. You can complete it within a year, market it before it's even finished, and send it out with reasonable hopes of seeing it in print within a few months. If need be, you can publish it yourself — and maybe get a regular publisher to sell it for you. You can do so without sacrificing your regular income, your family, or other activities.

I know you can, because I've done it. This book shows you how.

# PART 1: PLANNING

# 1

# Developing Efficient Work Habits

Different writers face different advantages and drawbacks in forming good writing habits. The circumstances of your personal life may make it easy or hard to find writing time, but time itself is not the real issue — it's *habit*.

Writing must be something you do regularly, like brushing your teeth. Wait for inspiration and you'll wait even longer for a complete, published book. The efficient writer exploits opportunity, but the best writing habits flourish in routine.

## Establishing a Routine

Set aside some time every day when you can work undisturbed for an hour or two. Times like first thing in the morning, during lunch, or after dinner are ideal. Choose a time when you can set aside other demands. Ideally, it should be at the same time each day.

Your family and friends will soon build their own routines around yours. If you are lucky, they will begin to notice your unscheduled appearances during your allotted writing time, and will send you packing back to your desk.

Keep your writing equipment (paper, pens, software manuals, etc.) in your writing place, close at hand. Try to find a writing time when few people phone or visit. Many authors have written books between 5:00 a.m. and waking their kids up. If a cup of coffee and some background music make you feel less lonely, by all means enjoy them.

Use household chores as thinking time. This is a perfect chance to review what you've done so far and to consider where your writing should go next. Walking the dog or vacuuming the carpet can provide more ideas than you expect.

This is really just "controlled daydreaming." Let your mind freewheel in a particular direction. Think about what the opening should be in the next chapter, or how to present both sides of a controversy. The process won't happen with nearly the same ease if you just sit and stare at the wall. You need to be up and moving in some automatic pattern in order to get your best thinking done. Being productive yields productivity!

Don't lean on others for editorial advice and encouragement, particularly those with whom you're emotionally involved. Spouses, friends, and roommates rarely have both the editorial skill and the tact to express their thoughts without infuriating you or breaking your heart. Empty praise will get you nowhere; unconstructive criticism can destroy your book in an instant.

Instead, be your own editor: set aside regular times to write yourself letters discussing your own work, articulating what's good and less good about it. In the process, you'll be able to solve small problems that could otherwise grow into full-blown writer's block.

On a computer, the letters can form a continuous journal, recording your reactions to the evolving work. Checking back to the first journal entries can help keep you on track of — or dramatically show how far you've moved from — your original concept.

Writing a letter to yourself is especially helpful if you're beginning to have anxiety about the book. Sometimes we try to suppress that anxiety, which only makes it worse. Anxiety turns to frustration and despair, and finally we abandon the whole project.

If you can actually write down what bothers you about your subject or your style, the answer to the problem often suggests itself. The act of turning our chaotic thoughts into orderly sentences seems to lead to much quicker and more satisfying solutions.

Here's a slightly scandalous tip: Don't respect text just because it's on the page. Just because you've written something doesn't mean it has a right to exist. If your internal editor can find a better way to say something, junk the original version and go with the new one. If you can't find a better way, and the passage really isn't good, junk it anyway and try again.

In addition to these self-addressed letters, keep a daily log of your progress. Word processors' word-count functions are powerful encouragers. The log can give you a sense of accomplishment, especially on big projects, and can enable you to set realistic completion deadlines.

For example, if you know you can write 500 words in an hour, and you write three hours a week, you can have a completed book manuscript of 75,000 words in 50 weeks. If you write ten hours a week, the manuscript will be complete in 15 weeks.

Compile a "project bible." This is a list of facts, names, and so on that you expect to be using for constant reference. If you have some important research findings you plan to use, put them in the bible along with their sources. If you don't have a laptop, the best format for this bible may be a loose-leaf binder you can carry with you. (A word of caution: If your bible gets too big to carry easily, its purpose is defeated.)

# Taking Advantage of Opportunity

If you decide you just can't write unless you're enthroned at your computer with Mozart on your iPod and no one else in the house, you're only making life harder for yourself.

Your routine will always contain "dead time" when you're away from home (or at least away from your workplace) with no other task at hand. You might be waiting in a doctor's office, on a bus, or trapped in a large, dull meeting.

By carrying your notebook bible, you can use that dead time constructively by recording at least a few lines of a rough draft. You might instead jot down some background notes about your project or a self-editing idea that's just occurred to you. You can then use these when you're back at your desk producing finished text.

These are general habits that will help you at all stages of the book-writing process. But you may also find that you need to understand those stages and adapt your habits to each of them. You won't do yourself any good if you plunge into the writing phase before you've worked out a decent outline.

In the following chapters, we'll take a look at the stages of planning your book, and then consider some techniques to maximize your efficiency in each of them.

# 2

# The Process of Publishing a Book

You've got an idea for a book. Now what?

If you understand the process of getting a book published, you can plan effectively, write quickly, and market efficiently. Let's look at the phases, bearing in mind that they usually overlap to some extent: You'll be writing in the planning phase, marketing while you're writing, and researching right up to the moment your book goes to press.

## The Planning and Research Phase

Write yourself a letter about the book. The letter should deal with at least some of the following issues:

- People — central characters, supporting characters; for instance, family members in memoirs or politicians and pioneers in a regional history

- Narrative — who did what, when, where, how, and, most importantly, why?

- Point of view — first-person narrator? Third-person limited? Third-person omniscient?

- Theme — does the story dramatize the temptations of political corruption? The joys of first love? The betrayal of idealism by a totalitarian state?

- Outcome — what do we and the characters learn by the end of the story? No politician escapes corruption? First love is never last love? Courage can defy the greatest tyrant?

Do a detailed outline/summary of the whole book, breaking it down into a section-by-section or chapter-by-chapter description. You can do this in sentences and paragraphs as straight narrative — the way you tell a friend about the events of the movie you saw last night — or you can describe each topic and event on a separate line, in the order they occur to you. Select each line and drag it to the beginning, middle, or end of your story. We'll look at this in more detail in Chapter 3, "Storyboarding."

If you know some of the material that's certainly going to be in the finished book, experiment by writing an article that can stand by itself. This will give you a good sense of your own writing speed; you will see how easy it can be to write 1,000 or 2,000 words.

Short articles are helpful even if you don't have a clear idea of the finished book. They're a form of "periscope writing," because they give you a sense of what you're getting yourself into. The articles themselves may surprise you by alerting you to issues you hadn't thought about, or don't know much about.

Research is also part of the planning process. It can be tedious and tiring, but some simple techniques of online research can help you turn up some amazing material. Finding it can be a thrill in itself, and then you'll want to tell the world about the surprises you've discovered.

# The Writing Phase

Write the first 100 pages of your manuscript (about 25,000 words). If you've already drafted some articles as part of your planning, incorporate them into the manuscript. As you progress, re-read your manuscript — the story will begin to reveal new insights as you re-read it upon which you can expand.

Keep writing editorial letters to yourself to see possible new lines of development in the story. Try not to go back and start from the top every time you get a new idea.

Minimize retyping and reprinting. A rough draft in longhand is easier to work on than a perfectly printed draft. Text on the computer screen is also much easier to revise, though some people do need paper in one hand and a pen in the other. If you have worked out your characters, narrative, point of view, theme, and outcome, rewriting should involve little beyond correcting typos or changing an occasional phrase.

# The Marketing Phase

Send a proposal/query letter along with the outline (and perhaps the first 100 pages) to a publisher. Research possible publishers to ensure that the publisher you're submitting to publishes books similar to yours. If your research has already turned up some useful books, their publishers should be on your shortlist. Most publishers' websites now give specific details about the kinds of books they're looking for and the way they want the manuscript to look.

Use any connection open to you to distinguish your manuscript from all the other unsolicited stuff. If you decide to get an agent first, the same advice applies: look for an agent who handles your kind of book, who knows the market you're trying to reach.

If the publisher/agent turns you down, find out why in as much detail as possible. Publishers don't usually say much unless they see a real possibility that a quick rewrite will result in a publishable book. Agents may supply detailed and useful critiques. Like publishers, they want to see a successful book.

Another possibility is to hire a freelance editor to read and scrutinize your manuscript. If the criticisms seem fair to you, revise your manuscript in accordance and send the revision out, either to the original publisher or to another house.

If the publisher likes your sample and outline —

- discuss details, revisions, terms of payment, and deadlines;

- go over the contract with the publisher, then with a lawyer or agent; and

- sign the contract (this may include payment of an advance, usually in thirds: a third on signing, a third on delivery of satisfactory manuscript, a third on publication).

## The Publishing Phase

Produce the book and deliver by the date specified in the contract. Deadlines are important. Expect (and hope for) extensive consultation over editing of the manuscript.

Copyediting happens in-house, but the corrected manuscript may come back to you. You are free to change back almost anything you don't like. But think carefully about it, because editors know what they're doing when they tinker with your prose.

Typesetting and art design will not normally involve you. You may get a copy of the cover art and you may have some say about the jacket copy. More likely, you won't.

Galleys or page proofs will reach you several weeks or months before publication date. Proofread and revise promptly but minimally. This is not the time to rewrite the whole book. Return only the pages that have corrections on them, by courier.

**Production and promotion:** Your book goes into the publisher's catalogue, and the publisher mentions you as a promising new writer at conferences with sales staff. Preview copies go out to reviewers, and the publisher touts the book at international book fairs.

**Publication (an often-arbitrary date):** The book is in the stores by this date.

**Author's promotion:** Talk shows, interviews, autographing. Not for all authors, but some do take this route if the publisher feels it'll help sales. Reason: It is cheaper to fly an author all over the country, cover hotel and travel costs, and hire PR firms to get the author on talk shows, than to take out a couple of big ads in *The New York Times* book-review section.

**Royalty statements:** These normally appear twice a year, 90 days or more after the close of the reporting period — April 1 for July-December, October 1 for January-June.

This may sound pretty simple, but some steps in the process can be slow and exhausting. Others may not apply to you. For example, your publisher may have no budget to send you out on tour. If so, your interviews will all be by phone or email, except for those in local media.

Now that you have a sense of what you're embarking on, you'll be able to move through the process knowing where the milestones are. Disappointments will turn up, but you'll be ready for them. And the successes will come sooner and faster, keeping you eager to complete your book.

# 3

## Storyboarding

"Storyboarding" usually means arranging a sequence of images for a film or commercial. Walt Disney created the term to help his animators work out the stages of a cartoon. But you can storyboard a book also, and it can be a helpful way to organize the material.

Human beings don't normally *think* in an organized way. We might have an idea for a family history, say, of the immigrant boy who founds a mining empire in Alberta wilderness, and a random assortment of mental images — Uncle Bill's snowbound winter, impact of the Depression, and some news clippings from the 1940s. How do we get from that to a coherent outline, and then to a book?

Here's one way to do it: Take a stack of 3x5 index cards and jot down an image or idea on each one, just in the order the ideas occur to you. It might look something like this:

> *Jesse arrives in Grande Cache, 1930(?)*
> *Meets future father-in-law, Douglas*
> *McRae, in June (source: family story).*

When you have 5 or 10 or 20 such cards, lay them out in the sequence you envisage for the story. You certainly don't have to have a card for each event or topic in the book, but you have the ones that your subconscious seems to want to deal with at the time.

You also have numerous gaps, which lead to useful questions. Where do you find Jesse's marriage certificate? Does Jesse's grandson still have any of his grandparents' correspondence? Are the family's property records still in Grande Cache or in Edmonton? Has anyone written a local history that might throw light on the general period and region?

New ideas will occur to you. That means more cards. Maybe some of the new ideas are better than the original ones, so some of the old cards may find their way into the recycling bin. New characters emerge to fulfill functions in the story. Your research into regional history suggests still more scenes which might go into this or that part of the book; still more cards go into your growing deck.

The story may eventually end up as a series of "theme" chapters, but for now stick to straight chronological order. Whatever the "real time" of your account, you may see that the cards clump naturally around certain periods, and you see no need to fill in the gaps. That's fine; maybe you've found the natural divisions between chapters or sections of the story.

Keep asking yourself *why* each element is going into your story. Don't keep an item in your storyboard unless you can justify it as a way to dramatize a character's personality, to move the story ahead, to lend verisimilitude, and so on. Although you may feel as though you absolutely must describe how Jesse's sister Sophia won a prize for her blueberry scones in Canmore in 1937, what good will the item do for the overall story?

Once you have at least the main sequence of events clearly mapped out on your cards, you can begin to transfer them into a more manageable synopsis or outline.

The same process is equally easy on a computer. Type the basics of the idea about Jesse arriving in Grande Cache. Hit the return key and type the next idea that occurs to you. Keep doing it until you (temporarily) run out of ideas.

Now select a particular idea and drag it to the top or bottom of the file, depending on whether it seems to belong to the beginning or end of the book. Do the same with another idea. Eventually you'll have a rough sequence of narrative or argument that you can use to build an outline.

Storyboarding works for both the overall structure of the book and for the organization of individual chapters or parts of chapters. So as you prepare to launch into Chapter 3 of your book, you may want to get out the 3x5 cards again to see what you should say and the sequence in which you should say it.

# 4

# Articles That Turn into Chapters

Writing articles on your subject can actually be part of the planning for your book. You can get a much more realistic sense of the work involved in the project, as well as learn where you'll need to do some extra research.

Equally important, it can provide you with a way to determine what your audience is, and how to write for it. If all goes well, you may even create an audience for the finished book which was not out there before.

If you're not concerned about money at this stage, your opportunities to publish are pretty good. Yes, many magazines and newspapers will pay good money for freelance articles. But those markets are fighting for their lives, and professional freelance writers are likely to outcompete you for the top-paying markets.

Other markets, however, are quite open to new writers with something special to say — as long as it doesn't cost them anything. This is especially true of periodicals serving local communities or specialized readerships.

Suppose, for example, you're writing a history of your town. The local weekly is likely to grab everything you offer it, especially if you supply it in well-organized articles of 500 to 1,200 words. Run those articles weekly or monthly, and readers will start looking forward to them (and maybe even sending you tips about local history that you can include in the book).

Or suppose you're writing on a specialized professional topic like real-estate law or running a veterinary practice. Some professional association is likely to welcome your articles for its newsletter or magazine, especially if you show you can keep producing them to a deadline. Again, you'll build up a readership and learn things you can use in your book.

Even more agreeably, when you develop a reputation among your readers as an entertaining authority, you may be invited to address meetings and conferences for the profession. This will widen your potential book market still more, and the honorariums may be substantial. (Your keynote speech or panel presentation may also be a good way to develop material for another chapter or two.)

If you're already reading your community weekly or some professional journals in your field, you're ahead of the game: You have a sense of the style and approach your market seems to prefer. But you may feel a bit intimidated because you're just starting your research, after all, and you're not even sure what to write about and how to do it.

# Finding Ideas

Here are some examples of types of articles and suggestions on how to find ideas for them.

Article topics divide into several major types. Some periodicals use all types; others specialize in a few or even just one. Thinking about specific types of articles is often more fruitful than trying to come up with just a topic.

1. The **think piece** helps readers understand and identify new trends, and to take a fresh look at topics they take for granted. The think

piece can be done on almost any topic, but it needs a fresh angle with new meaning. If your book deals with political, philosophical, or scholarly issues, it could yield a number of think-piece articles.

2. The **informative article** offers facts about something new, or something old that people don't know about. It can be anything from teenage slang to the history of a neighborhood. Almost any nonfiction book will include the materials for informative articles.

3. The **service article** advises readers on "how to" and "get going" subjects. It generally requires clear, step-by-step instructions and comparisons, based on your own experience or that of experts. If you're planning a book on how to sell your own home, a series of service articles on different parts of the process could appeal to many readers.

4. The **travel article** is often a blend of service and information; for instance, travel in Nepal is tough, and here's how to make it easier. A book on your globetrotting adventures across South Asia will include plenty of articles based on your hard-won experience.

5. The **personality profile** appeals to the gossip instinct. Many periodicals will take stories about unusual unknowns, like the aunts and uncles in your planned family memoir. The profile works best when it shows the ordinary side of the famous or the extraordinary side of the unknown.

6. The **personal experience** examines something in your life with wide relevance to others, for instance, coping with a rare or extremely common burden, or responding to a very ordinary or very bizarre experience. If you're writing a book on how to raise an autistic child, your own experience will carry great weight in a series of articles about key moments in your child's progress. Bear in mind that the personal experience article often requires a certain detachment, letting the event speak for itself.

And how do you get ideas that can work as both articles and chapters? Many ways!

- **Creative perversity:** Go against the received wisdom or climate of opinion. Debunk conventional attitudes, including your own, and see what your subject looks like from a very different angle.

- **Inquisitive naïveté:** Ask questions about what we usually take for granted: How do they make toothpicks, and where? How long does it take to grow a banana? Who got the idea for the computer mouse?

- **Brainstorm:** Bounce ideas off another person, without criticizing or rejecting any of them.

- **Solo brainstorm:** Write memos to yourself to focus your thoughts. You'll be amazed to see how fast the ideas come.

- **Anthropologize:** Study people's rituals, habits, and customs — not just in Nepal, but right in your home town.

- **Read and react:** What makes you happy or angry in the news these days? This is especially helpful if the news is on the subject of your book, and your articles, folded into the book, will help keep it timely.

- **Extrapolate:** If something goes on, what happens next? For example, the US Census estimates that in 2050 the American population 65 and older will number 78 million out of 393 million. How will America deal with that many seniors?

- **Compare/contrast:** A useful angle for stories on perennial topics: holidays, seasonal events, customs, etc. But you can also compare and contrast treatments for autism in, say, California and Portugal.

- **Go fishing:** Rummage through unfamiliar materials old newspapers, odd references, classified ads. If you know an important date in the history of your subject, check online newspaper archives to see what else was going on that day.

- **Appreciate:** Praise the merits of a rarely recognized person, place or thing.

- **Daydream:** Walk the dog, wash the dishes, and let your thoughts wander. You may come up with unexpected treasures.

# Article and Chapter Structure

The structure of a book chapter or article boils down to five syllables:

Hey! You! See? So — Ha!

In other words —

- attract interest in your opening sentences

- show how the subject concerns the reader

- discuss the subject in detail

- bring out the implications or consequences of what you've discussed

- come to a strong, satisfying conclusion

## The lede

Journalists deliberately misspell the word "lead" to avoid confusion with both the verb and the metal. The lede, or introduction, uses a "hook" that fits the mood of the chapter and links naturally with the body. The hook often introduces your most interesting, striking, or dramatic material.

## Lede devices

- **Anecdote:** A brief story, illustration, or example (real or fictitious) to spark interest and give a glimpse of the subject. Readers seem to realize that the anecdote will be short and will offer a quick reward for a few seconds' attention. For example, "Much to my surprise, I once encountered a bison on a road in Jasper National Park."

- **Question:** A general question, usually followed by the answer and the introduction of the subject. Readers will want to read further if the question is intriguing enough. For example, "What on earth was a bison doing in Jasper National Park?"

- **Unusual Statement:** Surprises the reader. Unusual statements can capture attention. For example, "He was a crusty old bachelor bison who'd taken a liking to the Rocky Mountains."

- **Summary Statement:** Condenses the essentials of the essay. For example, "Parks Canada officials sometimes experiment with the ecology of the Rocky Mountains by introducing unfamiliar species; the results aren't always happy."

- **Quotation:** An important, easily understood quotation that illustrates the subject and sets the mood of the piece. For some reason, readers seem to enjoy reading what someone actually said. For example, "'Oh, you saw him!' The Jasper Park naturalist looked both delighted and envious when I reported sighting a bison on the road to Celestine Lake."

- **Compare/contrast statements:** Past/future, male/female, good/bad, etc. For example, "Across the river, the highway to Edmonton was full of trucks; here on this single-lane dirt road, the only other traffic was one large black bison."

- **Direct Address:** Puts the reader imaginatively in the chapter. For example, "You may have seen bison in movies, but nothing can prepare you for the sight of a real one."

- **News peg:** Brings up an event related to the topic — not useful if the event will be ancient history by the time of publication. For example, "Recent reports of elk attacks in Banff show that humans and animals have not yet learned to coexist in the Rocky Mountain parks."

- **Allusion:** Direct or indirect reference to something readers are expected to know and understand. Keep in mind that if they don't understand the allusion, you have only succeeded in alienating your reader. For example, "Meeting a bison in Jasper Park wasn't anything like the hunt in *Dances with Wolves*."

- **Rebuttal:** Contradiction of something said or reported. This promises a conflict, and readers love conflict. For example, "Despite what some writers assert, no bison live in Jasper National Park."

The lede must not only interest the reader; it must also outline the limits and direction of your chapter and express a thesis, or major assertion, about your topic.

If you plan to discuss mountain goats and grizzlies as well as bison, you'd better say so early; otherwise you'll startle the reader when you drop the subject of bison and go on to seemingly unrelated topics. This forecast and thesis may require only a single sentence, or as much as a couple of paragraphs. For instance: "This casual encounter was the direct result of Parks Canada policies which could affect bison and every other species in the Rocky Mountains, especially mountain goats, grizzlies, and human beings. By conducting misguided 'experiments,' Parks Canada could be endangering the very animals it is supposed to protect."

This paragraph offers a number of unspoken "promises" to the reader: In this chapter I will give you an exposition of Parks Canada policies; I will cite examples of these policies and how they affect mountain goats, grizzlies, and humans; I will argue that Parks Canada policies on this subject need to be changed.

Once your readers know what you plan to tell them, they'll relax and deal with each topic as it comes.

## The body

Organization of your article or chapter can be:

- Logical (assertion, evidence, conclusion)
- Narrative (this happened, then that happened)
- Categorical (five ways to lose weight fast; four causes of student failure)

Many styles blend all three to some extent. Each paragraph should —

- have a smooth, clear transition from the last paragraph;
- express a central idea or topic, usually stated in a topic sentence, with further sentences to explain, prove, illustrate, or summarize;
- be concise, clear, and appropriate in tone; and
- prepare the reader for the next paragraph.

### Hypotaxis or parataxis?

The technical term for this kind of organization is "hypotaxis," where ideas have clear links or transitions to other ideas. Most readers are grateful for this kind of guidance.

But another kind of organization has its advantages. "Parataxis" puts ideas side by side without transitions. This can be confusing, but if readers can make the connection themselves, the impact is enormous. If you make a key point in the lede, and then you allude to it in the body without a reminder or transition, it can have a powerful effect. This is what wit is all about: The sudden linkage of two seemingly unrelated ideas.

Parataxis is also the basis of the climax of a mystery story, when the detective reminds us of some critical bit of evidence that points inarguably to the real criminal. We instantly jump to the desired conclusion: *Of course! Why didn't I think of that?*

In general, your article or chapter should rely mostly on the clear transitions of hypotactic writing. But an occasional jolt of parataxis can surprise and delight your readers.

However you choose to organize it, tell your story as clearly as possible, using whatever devices will make it lively: anecdotes, quotations, unusual statements, and so on.

In other words, lede devices are also devices to sustain interest throughout the body of the chapter. Start with a quotation, and include more quotations. Ask a question, and then ask another question. Sprinkle anecdotes through the whole article. By giving your readers a series of rewards, you keep them hooked.

## The ending

The ending needs a "kicker" — a statement that brings your article or chapter to a definite close. The kicker often uses lede devices inversely, to link with the opening paragraphs: anecdote for anecdote, quotation for quotation.

So if you start a chapter about airline safety with an anecdote about your Aunt Agatha's fear of flying, you might close by referring to her again. If you start with a proverb or quotation from Shakespeare, remind your readers at the end by mentioning the proverb or quoting Shakespeare again — maybe with a very different meaning.

That's why they call it a kicker; the paratactic impact is so strong that readers will say "Ha!" as they make the connection.

If one purpose of your chapter is to stir your readers to action, your lede device could illustrate the danger of doing nothing. The kicker at the end, by reminding readers of the hazards of apathy, can lend extra energy to your call to arms — and encourage readers to turn to the next chapter for more surprises and excitement.

# Approaching Editors

Ideally, you already know the periodicals (print and online) that might be interested in your articles. You can also do Google searches (see Chapter 6) that may turn up potential markets. To get a sense of what the online periodicals offer, see the list on the right-hand side of the page of my blog: http://crofsblogs.typepad.com/nonfiction.

A hundred years ago, aspiring writers were supposedly terrified of meeting real live editors. A shy novice wouldn't even open the door to the magazine's office; the poor wretch would toss a manuscript over the transom, a ventilation window above the door.

Ever since, the expression "over the transom" has been used to describe an unsolicited article from an unknown writer. Such submissions will sometimes get published, but professionals don't waste their time writing a complete article without editorial approval — it's like cooking a meal for ten and hoping ten friends will drop by in time for dinner.

Still, if you've written an article or two as part of your planning, you might as well query some editors about them.

Query letters were once, of course, purely postal. Now email has largely replaced postal correspondence. Both have their uses. In the 1990s, an email query was still unusual, and editors responded promptly. Then every freelance writer in the world began sending email queries, often with attached manuscripts, and editors lost their enthusiasm. (Attachments with viruses didn't help.)

So, ironically, an old-fashioned postal query could get more attention than the same message sent by email. The letter on paper seems to say, "I took the trouble to print this because I care so much about my subject."

Many periodicals have instructions on their websites about how to submit a query. If your intended market is one of them, follow what they say — whether they want email or postal mail.

The content, in either medium, is going to be like a mini-article: You'll attract the attention and interest of a distracted and overworked editor, pitch your idea, and end with a kicker, or at least a good-will message. See Example 1 for a sample query in postal-letter format.

# EXAMPLE 1: POSTAL QUERY LETTER

| | |
|---|---|
| Arthur Author<br>1234 Grub Street<br>Vancouver BC V6H 2F6<br>Phone: (604) 993-5678 Fax (604) 993-5679<br>aauthor@shaw.ca | Return Address |
| September 21, 2010<br><br>Mr. Herb Linguini, Editor<br>*Rocky Mountain Magazine*<br>PO Box 1445<br>Edmonton AB<br>T5E 1T6 | Inside address |
| Dear Mr. Linguini, | |
| He was a crusty old bachelor bison who'd taken a liking to life in the Rocky Mountains. When I ran into him by chance on a Jasper Park back road, I didn't expect to learn about Parks Canada's quiet experiments in wilderness ecology—but finding out why he was there soon led to a host of other questions. | Opening paragraph tries to hook editor, then leads into summary of article. |
| Surprisingly, Parks Canada routinely introduces species to habitats where they don't normally live, and then tracks their success or lack of it. In the case of the bison, a whole herd either died in the park or soon migrated back to the prairies. Critics might wonder whether this was the best possible use of taxpayers' dollars. | |
| Would you be interested in seeing, on spec, an article about this practice and its consequences? I would draw upon a number of Parks Canada reports, interviews with parks officials, at least one academic ecologist, and other experts like Ben Gadd, author of *The Rocky Mountain Handbook*. The article, tentatively titled "Buffaloed in Jasper," would run about 2500 words and I could complete it within three weeks. Some digital photos are also available. | Pitch includes info sources to lend authenticity. |
| As a longtime visitor to Jasper, I closely follow policies affecting the park. I have written a number of articles on the park and related issues, and I have good contacts in Parks Canada. I'm currently working on a book about issues in the Rocky Mountain parks. | Author includes his or her own credentials. |
| If you don't find this article of interest at the moment, perhaps I could suggest "Jasper's Secret Treasures"—a piece on little-known regions of the park that can make a visit even more memorable. I look forward to your response. Best wishes for the continued success of *Rocky Mountain Magazine!* | Author suggests alternative article, closes on a friendly note. |
| Sincerely<br><br>*Arthur Author*<br><br>Arthur Author | |

Obviously, you won't follow Example 1 word for word, but the structure should give you something to go on. Some queries even use the lede of the article, on the assumption that a good hook will please the editor. But whatever first paragraph you write, it should convey competence, expertise, and enthusiasm for your subject.

The expression "on spec" is short for "on speculation": You're speculating that the editor will buy the article after a free look. Otherwise, the assumption is that if the editor says he or she will look at it, you've been commissioned and can expect payment. Editors don't like to do that until they know and trust you.

Note also that the letter includes a brief alternative pitch at the end. Generations of freelance writers have learned that you don't pitch an editor with just one idea.

If you're really impatient and you want to send the whole article over the transom, it still needs a cover letter. It might look something like Example 2.

As a postal letter, this includes an enclosure notation mentioning the title of the article. If you send an email query, however, don't attach the article — because of the risk of viruses, editors tend to delete emails with attachments unless they know the sender. So you might simply paste the article into the email itself.

## Article Format

If you send an article as just a text file, format doesn't matter much. Some editors don't mind working with text on a computer screen, but many still prefer to work with a hard copy that they can scribble on. As with your eventual book editor, your task with your periodical editor is to make his or her job as easy as possible. So if you submit your article as a word-processed document to be printed off, follow a format that makes the editor comfortable. As we'll see, format for the book manuscript is very similar.

Note, in Example 3, that you include your name as you want to see it on the check, but your byline can be something different. The article length is usually rounded off to the nearest hundred words.

# EXAMPLE 2: LETTER WITH SUBMISSION

Jo Doakes
1234 Downs Street
North Vancouver BC V7G 1H7
Phone 604-555-3003 | Fax 604-555-3449
email jdoakes@intergate.ca

September 15, 2010

Ms Joanne Smith, Editor
*The Shore*
#23, 1501 Lonsdale
North Vancouver BC V7M 2J2

Dear Ms Smith

Enclosed is a thousand-word article for your consideration titled, "Should We Shut Down the Baden-Powell Trail?" The trail is so popular that the traffic is damaging it. While North Shore parks officials have made considerable efforts to restore and maintain it, the impact of thousands of hikers and bikers is causing erosion and pollution problems. The problem is completely avoidable, since our mountains offer many other challenging trails.

I've walked the Baden-Powell many times myself, and spoken with scores of other hikers. In addition, I interviewed Julie Patterson of North Vancouver District Parks, to get her side of the story. The article comes out of research I'm doing for a book on the trails of the North Shore.

Whether or not you find this piece suitable, I'd be grateful for your comments. Best wishes for your magazine's continued success!

Sincerely

*Jo Doakes*


encl
"Should We Shut Down the Baden-Powell Trail?"

# EXAMPLE 3: ARTICLE FORMAT

Josephine Doakes
1234 Downs Street
North Vancouver BC V7G 1H7
Phone: 604-929-3003 | Fax 604-929-3449
email jdoakes@shaw.ca

1500 words

### ARTICLE TITLE IN CAPS

By Jo Doakes

Your text begins one double-space below your byline. Indent each paragraph half an inch from the left-hand margin. Margins should be 2.5 to 3 cm (1" to 1-$\frac{1}{2}$") all around. Use 21x28 cm (8-$\frac{1}{2}$"x11") white paper.

Double-space your manuscript, and use a standard typeface; never use *script* or **bold** typefaces, and save italics for *emphasis*. Keep a ragged right margin. Proofread on paper, not from the screen; the manuscript you submit should have no handwritten corrections.

Following pages should carry a header like this:

Doakes                                                                                              2


Resume text two double-spaces below the header. Try to avoid beginning a paragraph on the last line of the page ("widows"), or ending a paragraph on the first line of a page ("orphans").

Submit the manuscript with pages in order but not clipped or stapled together. If the manuscript is over five or six pages, mail it flat. Don't forget a covering letter describing the article and your qualifications for writing it. If you fax the manuscript, page numbers should indicate total length: Page 2 of 6, Page 3 of 6, etc. If you email the manuscript, send it as a text file (ASCII) unless you know the editor has the same word processor that you do and will accept emailed attachments. Single-spaced text is all right for emailed text files, but double-space between paragraphs.

The End

# 5

# The Business of Writing

What if you actually do complete and sell your book — and it even makes some money? That happy event catches a lot of writers by surprise; I was one of them. A couple of my early books made more money than I'd ever imagined, and I was suddenly dealing with literary fame and exciting tax problems.

Whether you realize it or not, as a writer you're also a small-business person. You have to spend money to make money, and your government is prepared to give you some tax breaks to help you stay in business. To maximize those breaks, you should start planning now for writing income that may not come in for several years.

Even before you are selling, you can deduct costs of writing and research from your taxable income just like the owner of any other small start-up business, but you must keep good records. Consult a tax accountant to ensure that you qualify as a writer and that your deductions are legitimate.

In Canada, you can usually qualify as a writer if you meet the following federal guidelines:

- You can document the time you devote to writing and research as compared to your other occupation. So start keeping a written record of your research now. Your ongoing letter to yourself should be adequate if you're noting, for example, time spent today in online research.

- You can list the extent and nature of your published works. This is another advantage of writing and marketing articles that you will eventually incorporate into the book.

- Your writing is for general sale rather than restricted distribution, like writing done as part of your regular job.

- You can supply the name of your publisher (or proof of efforts to publish, like copies of query letters and book proposals).

- You can offer your plans for future writing, including works in progress.

- You can list your anticipated revenue from royalties, rights sales, and government grants.

- You can document your expenses for research, writing, and promotion. If you had to pay your state archives for permission to use some photos of your town in 1910, hold on to the receipt. The same applies to secretarial and editorial help, book-related travel costs, and so on.

- You can document efforts to promote the sale of your works — for example, by sending out review copies of a self-published book, or travel costs incurred to do an interview on a radio or TV station.

- You can show your qualifications as a writer: your education, honors, awards, grants, etc. This may not be critical if your book on fly fishing is based on your personal fishing experience.

- You can document the significance and growth of your writing income: If your articles didn't pay anything, and your book didn't either, you have a poor case for deducting writing expenses. You may be able to deduct expenses for a few years, but if you show continuous losses, the tax people will eventually decide you're a hobbyist, not a professional, and tax you accordingly.

- You can document external factors affecting sales (for example, your publisher's bankruptcy).

If you meet the tax criteria as a writer, you have a lot of allowable expenses that you can deduct from your other income. These expenses may include:

- stationery supplies;

- postage and courier charges;

- computer, office furniture and equipment (including repairs), software, photocopying (leased equipment is entirely deductible; purchased equipment is usually deductible on a multi-year depreciation basis);

- long-distance telephone calls, fax, Internet account;

- photos, maps, charts, etc. used to illustrate manuscripts;

- editing, secretarial services, research and copyright fees, accounting services, legal and agent's fees, insurance on library and equipment (so if you hire a freelance editor to go over your manuscript, you can deduct the fee from your taxable income. The same applies to what your accountant charges you);

- books of any kind; magazine and newspaper subscriptions used in connection with writing. If you're writing a book in your professional field, the cost of subscribing to your professional journals and newsletters should be deductible;

- union or association dues; fees for courses or conventions related to writing. If you qualify to join The Writers' Union of Canada, or you take a course in nonfiction writing at your local university, those costs are also deductible;

- office rental; an in-home office used only for writing may qualify you for pro-rata deduction of mortgage, taxes, insurance, heat and light, etc. Check with your accountant to make sure you qualify; and

- gifts, travel and entertainment expenses necessary to your work, including vehicle mileage (requires a detailed log of trips taken on business). Self-publishers should pay special attention to this: If you're driving from bookstore to bookstore with a trunk full of copies to place on consignment, keep track of your mileage.

If you are in the US, many of these general ideas do still apply. Check with your accountant to make sure you are recording expenses and deductions properly.

Again, your personal circumstances may help or hurt your tax status as a writer. Don't take my advice on this, but do consult a good accountant or tax lawyer to make sure you maximize your tax breaks. And do it now, long before you actually start marketing your manuscript.

# PART 2:
# RESEARCH

# 6

# Researching on the Web

So far, most of the suggestions I've offered could have been followed in the age of the typewriter, or of the quill pen. But you're working in the best environment that writers have ever known — one in which you can draw on an astonishing wealth of resources for planning, researching, writing, and marketing your work.

To exploit these resources, you need some basic computer skills, or at least someone who can help you go online and show you where to start looking. For the purposes of this chapter, I'll assume that you can create a word-processed document and that you know how to use a browser like Mozilla Firefox or Internet Explorer, but I won't assume that you know much about how to use Google, the major search engine. We'll start there.

# The Basic Google Window

Here's the window that most people see when they go searching for something on the web:

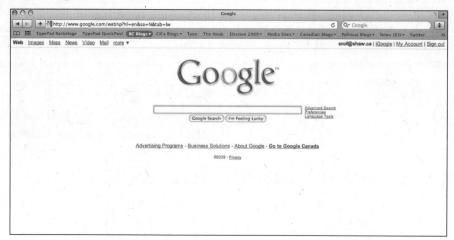

Notice in the upper left-hand corner you have links to **Images, Maps, News, Video, Mail,** and **more.** You may want to use some or all of these resources later on, but "more" will lead you to the real paydirt. We'll come back to that in a little while.

In the center of the screen is the Google logo and search window, with two buttons: **Google Search** and **I'm Feeling Lucky.** Ignore them.

Below the buttons are links to **Advertising Programs, Business Solutions, About Google,** and **Go to Google.** (Since I live in Canada, that button takes me to Google.ca. Wherever you live, Google will normally take you to your national Google page.) You may well want to learn more about advertising with Google later on, but that can wait.

Just to the right of the search box are three crucial links: **Advanced Search, Preferences,** and **Language Tools.** These will help you customize Google Search to serve you better.

## Advanced Search

When you click on **Advanced Search,** you find several windows plus buttons and more links. Let's go through the first three search boxes.

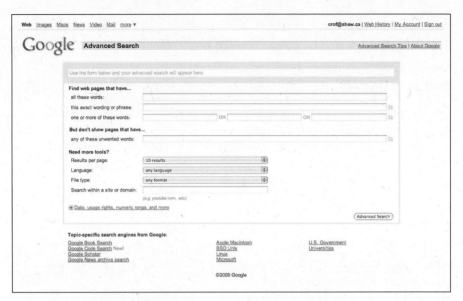

**All these words:** Here you can type in any words you think will help you find what you're looking for. If you're working on a history of Jefferson County, Missouri, you could type those three words in here.

However, this search will find every file with the word Jefferson, the word County, and the word Missouri. Google will find millions of pages with those words, and very few of them will be what you're looking for.

You can get around this, however, by putting quotes around the words: Typing in, "Jefferson County Missouri" will tell Google to search for those three words in sequence. (You don't even need to use capital letters.)

**This exact wording or phrase:** In this window, you don't need to bother with the quotation marks. Just type in a name, a phrase, or even a whole sentence, and Google will find it.

What if you want to look for two phrases at the same time? Just type one phrase in quotes in the top window, and the other without quotes in the middle window.

**One or more of these words:** Here you can look for additional words that can focus your search. If you do Google "Jefferson County Missouri," you'll probably get over 36,000 hits — too many to go through individually. But if you add, say, a family name to the search, Google will turn up just the pages that mention the county and the family.

**But don't show pages that have … :** This tells Google to avoid pages with any term you don't want at all.

Now look at the **Need more tools?** section of the window. You can specify how many results per page, or hits, Google should display in a window. Ten hits per page is the default, but you can set it for up to 100 hits before clicking to the next page of hits. Yes, it takes Google a split-second longer to post a 50-hit page, but you probably won't notice the difference.

You can also specify the language of the pages you're searching. **Any language** is the default, and you'll probably leave it there, but if you know that the resources you want are in Bulgarian or Catalan, you can limit the search to that language.

You can also specify the file type. Maybe you want only PDF files, or only Word files, or only Excel spreadsheet files.

**Search within a site or domain** is another opinion. If you're looking for YouTube clips, or articles on Canadian (.ca) websites only, this is where you can specify these limits.

If you click on the link to **Date, usage rights, numeric range, and more**, you will find still more options.

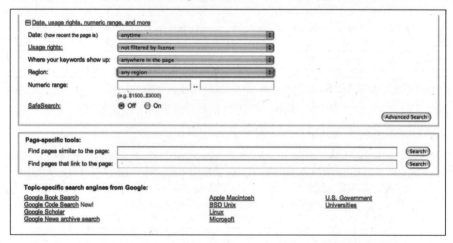

**Date** lets you specify how recent the page should be, from "anytime" to "the last 24 hours."

With **Usage rights**, you can filter Google's results by the freedom that users are granted to modify or change what they find. The default, not filtered by license, is probably your best bet.

You can select whether your key words show up in the page, or the title, or the URL.

**Region** permits you to focus on a specific country. **Numeric range** is very convenient for narrowing down time spans or price ranges: For example, Canadian politics 1867-1897, or digital cameras, $300-$700.

**SafeSearch** tells Google not to display text or graphics that may be pornographic. You probably won't need to turn SafeSearch on unless you're sharing your computer with a child, or you're using search terms that have led Google to show you pornographic sites.

Google then gives you even more useful resources on this page: page-specific tools, and topic-specific search.

Suppose you've discovered a really good website dealing with the history of Jefferson County. You can copy the URL (the web address) from the address bar at the top of your browser, paste it into the **Find pages similar to the page** box, and click the Search button (or just hit the Return key). When I did that for the blog of this book (http://crofsblogs.typepad.com/nonfiction), I got 30 hits, some of them to my own blogs, but most to other writing sites.

When I pasted the URL of another of my blogs into the second window, **Find pages that link to the page**, I found 879 pages with links to it.

For topic-specific searches, Google gives you still more tools: **Book Search** lets you search the text of thousands of books online, **Code Search** lets you find computer code, **Scholar** covers academic and scholarly pages, and **News Archive** turned up 37 hits for "Crawford Kilian" — including a 1969 *New York Times* review of my first publication, a children's book.

In addition, you can use four search engines designed to find information about particular computer operating systems: Apple Macintosh, BSD Unix, Linux, and Microsoft.

# Customizing Google

Now that you know the basic functions of Advanced Search, you can set your own preferences. This will make searching much faster and more effective.

Go back to the Google home page and click on the Preferences link beside the search box.

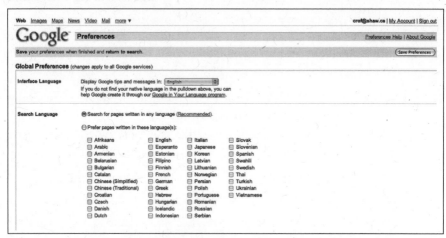

At the top of the Preferences window, you can select the **Interface language** — the language that Google uses for offering advice and results. English is probably your choice.

Then select the **Search Language**. Google recommends searching for pages written in any language, and I agree. But you may find some searches work better in a specific language. A book on the politics of Thailand may need more research in Thai-language sources than in English.

The bottom of the page gives you more choices:

Here's where you can set **Safesearch**. I recommend "Do not filter," but you may prefer moderate (no graphics) or strict (no text, no images).

Set your default **Number of Results** to more than 10 — I find 50 results per page works well. It's not that much slower, and you can scan the results more easily.

Displaying your hits in a new **Results Window** is also helpful. You can close that window and be back on the page where you started without having to click the "Back" button several times.

If you ask Google to provide **Query Suggestions**, it will try to guess what you're searching for as soon as you start typing, and offer a drop-down menu of possible terms. If the term you're typing is on the list, you can just click on it and save yourself the typing. (You'll also get a list of your recent searches, whether or not your current search involves those terms.)

Click the **Save** button in the lower-right corner, and you're in business. (You may need to go to your browser preferences to enable cookies before the Google preferences will work. A "cookie" is a kind of identification that many websites require. Some computer users prefer to disable cookies for reasons of privacy, but it's not worth the trouble.)

With your preferences set, go back to the Advanced Search page. In the address bar at the top, you'll see the URL of the Advanced Search page. You can now bookmark this page for a quick link to Google Advanced Search, configured the way you want it.

For example, suppose you find a word you don't know, like "magma." Click on your Advanced Search icon, and in any of the "Find web pages that have … " windows, type *define: magma*. Hit the return key or search button, and you'll get close to 400 definitions! (The first one should be enough.)

Note: If you use a colon, you get differently presented results than you will if you just type "define magma." Also, this command works in the regular Google search bar, whether or not you've set up advanced search.

# More Google Search Tools

You'll see the links across the top of most Google pages: **Images, Maps, News, Video, Mail**, and **more**. You can customize search tools like **Images** and **Maps** also, and even **News**. The one to pay attention to now is **more**. Click on the blue arrow beside it, and a drop-down menu appears with links to **Groups, Books, Scholar**, and so on. You can explore some of these resources on your own. At the bottom, however, is **even more>>**; click on that, and a whole range of tools will open up.

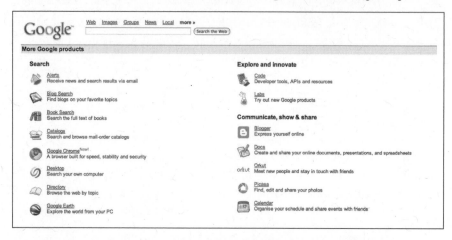

The image shows just part of what's on the page (as of this book going to press), but several of the search tools can be invaluable.

With **Alerts**, you can ask Google to keep a constant watch for terms that you're interested in. Maybe a journalist is writing excellent articles on your topic. Create a Google Alert for that journalist's name, and Google will email you every time he or she publishes a new story or is mentioned on the web.

Or if you're researching a particular company, a Google Alert will bring you every new story and news release about that company. You can set the terms of an alert — for example, to search only News, or only Blogs — and you can specify delivery of alerts to be once a day, once a week, or "as-it-happens." When you no longer need news on a topic, it's easy to cancel the alert for it.

**Blog Search** is also helpful. With millions of blogs, many of them on obscure subjects, Blog Search finds just the ones you want. As usual, you can set your own preferences, and you can also specify a particular time, such as between 15 April 2009 and 20 April 2009. When millions of blogs are being updated every day, it's really helpful to focus on narrow time periods.

Since Google has started to put thousands of books online, you can also use **Book Search** to find references. Go to **Advanced Book Search**, type in "Thai politics," and you get at least partial access to over 500 books that use the term.

**Google Directory** harks back to the early days of the web, when searching by categories was almost the only way to find things.

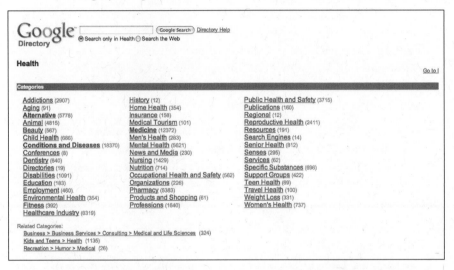

Clearly, narrowing down your topic to "Medical Tourism" or "Home Health" will still give you almost more links than you can handle. But **Directory** may also give you surprising and useful new leads for your research.

If your subject is a scholarly one, you will find **Google Scholar** a wonderful help. It searches through academic journals, theses, books, and abstracts.

As you can see, Google Scholar lets you find articles by a particular author, or from a particular journal, within a particular time period. You can also specify articles from various scientific and economic disciplines. Google Scholar works very well with the humanities as well.

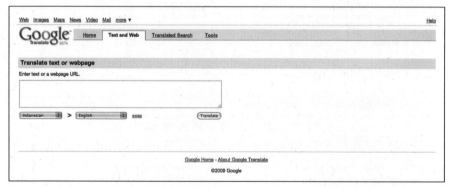

Finding a scholarly article doesn't always mean easy access to it. Many journals publish online, but limit readers to their subscribers — and subscriptions are usually very expensive. Even a single article may cost you a substantial amount of money.

However, you can usually see at least the abstract of the article, which should be enough for you to decide if the article is absolutely essential to your research. If it is, and you can't afford to buy it, you may at least be able to track down a hard copy of the journal in your local college or university library.

You aren't even limited to the languages you know. Google can certainly find materials in other languages that may be of value, and you can then use **Google Translate** to get a sense of what the materials are saying.

Note that you can copy and paste in a chunk of selected text, or just put the URL in and get a "machine translation" of the whole web page into any of over 40 languages. But don't expect a perfect rendition! Here's a translation into Spanish of my text about Google Scholar:

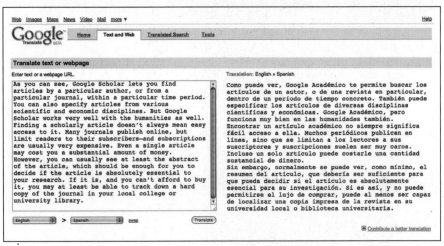

My own Spanish is a bit rusty, but even I can see that the translation is rough and awkward in places. As with a scholarly abstract, you can get the gist of the passage and learn something from it.

Clearly, Google has transformed the way we do research. But it's not the only way, and sometimes it's not even the best way. Old-fashioned library research is still critical, and so is interviewing — especially face-to-face interviews with your sources.

# 7

# Researching in Libraries

Libraries were once the only places you could do serious book research, especially on scholarly topics, because only the libraries had substantial holdings. They're still extremely useful, in part because you can reach them online as well as in person.

Let's look at what the libraries at a couple of universities have to offer: Capilano University, where I taught for 40 years, and Columbia University in New York City.

Most college and university libraries will serve members of the public as well as students and faculty, and Capilano is one of them. When you visit its Library page, you see a number of links. Let's go through them.

## Online Catalogue

Here you can search the library holdings, including not only books but also periodicals, videos, and CDs. You can search by the title, author,

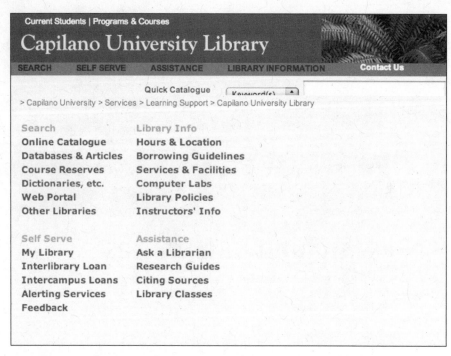

Current Students | Programs & Courses

Capilano University Library

SEARCH     SELF SERVE     ASSISTANCE     LIBRARY INFORMATION     Contact Us

Quick Catalogue   Keyword(s)
> Capilano University > Services > Learning Support > Capilano University Library

Search
Online Catalogue
Databases & Articles
Course Reserves
Dictionaries, etc.
Web Portal
Other Libraries

Library Info
Hours & Location
Borrowing Guidelines
Services & Facilities
Computer Labs
Library Policies
Instructors' Info

Self Serve
My Library
Interlibrary Loan
Intercampus Loans
Alerting Services
Feedback

Assistance
Ask a Librarian
Research Guides
Citing Sources
Library Classes

keyword, or subject heading. This gives you a good chance of stumbling across resources you didn't even know existed.

You can also go fishing by entering a Library of Congress (LC) number. For example, PS means English literature, and 5398 means Mary Shelley, who wrote *Frankenstein*. If you find an LC number about one work that's useful to you, type it into the library's search box and see what else it can find.

University libraries often hold "course reserves" of textbooks used for specific courses. If your book is about regional history, your local post-secondary institution may run courses with invaluable resources for your book. Such resources are usually reserved for students, but at least you know they exist.

# Databases and Articles

Here you can start tracking materials by topic or academic discipline, from fine arts to law to medicine. You can also browse databases by subject (but be aware that Capilano lists subjects taught in its programs, and other schools may have different lists).

## Dictionaries, etc.

That's a big "et cetera"! This link will take you to a wide range of reference materials, from maps to quotations to encyclopedias.

## Web portal

This is a convenient way to find online resources that may supplement research in Capilano University's subjects.

## Other libraries

While this page provides links mostly to academic and public libraries in the Vancouver region, it can also take you to national and world library networks. It's often possible to track down a resource to a specific library and then arrange for an interlibrary loan.

> Be sure to **Ask a Librarian** if you run into trouble or just want to speed up your research. Academic librarians, like their public-library colleagues, are amazingly knowledgeable about their holdings, and skilled at finding what they don't necessarily have at their fingertips.

When you visit the Columbia University Libraries at www.columbia. edu/cu/lweb, you'll see some similar services. But you will soon realize you're in a far larger and more complex environment. You'll even need a map to find where the libraries are (the website supplies such a map).

You'll also find a wide range of "E-Resources," including full-text books and journals, images, and scholarly documents created by Columbia faculty. Click on the arrow to the "newest E-Resources," and you'll see still more valuable collections.

As with Capilano, you can also ask Columbia librarians for advice and assistance, and you should be able to create your own account with the libraries — enabling you to search their catalogs.

Finally, visit the Library of Congress at www.loc.gov. Here you're dealing with such an enormous resource that it's broken down into categories based on the kind of visitor: kids and families, publishers, researchers, and so on. Budget plenty of time to explore it.

# In-Person Library Research

It's likely that you'll have to do some in-person library research. If you've familiarized yourself with online library resources, you should be able to get the most out of even your small branch library. And when you introduce yourself to the local librarians, and explain what you're doing, they're likely to do some research on your behalf, and send you tips about what they've found.

Among the other resources available, you'll likely find microfilm and microfiche useful. Microfilm puts thousands of pages on a reel of film that runs through a reader. Microfiche uses postcard-sized film with several dozen pages per fiche.

While many documents that were once limited to microfilm are now available online, access is often limited or expensive. But most libraries have extensive holdings on microfilm, and it's usually possible to print out useful material. (As with photocopies, such printouts will cost you a few cents per page. Keep a record of what you spend; it may be tax deductible.)

As well, you may accidentally run across other useful materials that you might otherwise never find: a local newspaper story from 1943 that mentions your grandmother and also runs a "house for sale" ad that gives you an idea of what the family's house was worth back then. Such connections can give you a deeper sense of the atmosphere of the time.

In-person research can also help you find scholarly articles that have never been put online (or are expensive to purchase). Even if your library doesn't have the article, it may be able to obtain a photocopy of it for you.

# 8

# Building an Online Workspace

If you have some basic computer skills, you have a couple of options for online research and writing.

The simplest is just to turn on your browser, use Google to find some useful websites, and bookmark those sites. You can organize the sites into folders if you wish, and install the folders in the browser toolbar. Then, if you want to visit the Library of Congress or Columbia University Libraries, they're accessible at once.

When you find a useful document this way, you can add it to your collection by bookmarking it, too. If it's a PDF file, it may be simpler to download it to a folder on your desktop. If so, feel free to give the download a clear and obvious name — many PDFs have meaningless names.

This method is pretty straightforward, and may be all you need. But if you've got a lot of research materials, it may become increasingly hard to find a particular website or document. You may have folders within folders, and just keeping the resources organized can become a full-time job. (If you're like me, you may also find that you haven't really read and absorbed the materials you've bookmarked — instead, you've just stashed them away in a folder!)

Another organization method is to create a blog as a workspace. This may seem like even more work, but blogging has become increasingly easy, and a blog dedicated to research and writing can then turn into a tool for marketing the finished book.

When I agreed to write a second edition of my book about the black pioneers of British Columbia, the first thing I did was to create a blog for it (http://crofsblogs.typepad.com/pioneers/). Here's a screenshot of part of the home page:

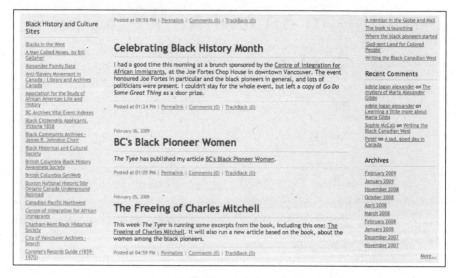

Notice especially the links in the left-hand column under "Black History and Culture Sites." I used some of them, such as the BC Archives Vital Event Indexes, almost every day. If I found a particular pioneer's name, I could go to the Vital Event Indexes, run the name, and see if that person had been born, baptized, married, or buried in British Columbia. (Marriage records were especially useful, because the spouse became someone else to research.)

Similarly, British Columbia Genweb is a site for genealogical research that I used again and again. It includes nineteenth-century census data, city directories, and voters' lists — even the deaths of convicts between 1875 and 1916. So I could click back and forth between, say, a voters' list and the Vital Events Index, learning about a voter's family and then tracking the family members as well.

What's more, when I found a useful site, I could add it to the Black History and Culture Sites list, and then consult it quickly and easily whenever I wanted to.

The middle column of the Pioneers blog was another kind of workspace. Here I could keep a log of my progress on the book, mentioning problems and successes, and also posting links to the articles about the pioneers that I was publishing in *The Tyee*. Once the book was actually published, the blog became a means to promote the book.

In the same way, I created a blog for this very book (http://crofsblogs.typepad.com/nonfiction), where I could keep an occasional diary about progress and present a great many links useful to me and to buyers of the book. I encourage you to check out the blog for more information on what I've written in this book.

## Designing a Book Blog

I don't consider myself a very computer-savvy person, but gaining basic blog skills is simple. If you want to create an online workspace in the form of a blog, you can do it very cheaply. If a basic blog makes it easier for you to produce your book, you'll find good reasons to add more bells and whistles.

You can start a blog free at Blogger (www.blogger.com), and work your way step-by-step into a usable site. You can also build a blog at TypePad (www.typepad.com), where you can set up a 14-day free-trial blog. If you're happy with the results, you can choose one of three types of accounts, the cheapest of which costs only about $5 a month.

To create a temporary, free TypePad blog, go to the TypePad home page at www.typepad.com. Click on the "Free Trial" button and follow the instructions. You'll need a valid credit card, but you won't have to pay anything until and unless you decide to make this a permanent account.

While I started with Blogger, most of my experience is with Type-Pad. So I'll discuss the components of a book blog as you can create them with TypePad. (If you have better computer skills than I do, you may want to use WordPress, a slighty more sophisticated application available at www.wordpress.com.)

## Starting your blog

When you begin, you give your blog a name and you acquire a URL (web address) for it. You can choose to make it public, which means TypePad's home page will display a link to your site every time you publish a post on it. If you would rather work in private, you can do so. You can even password-protect your site.

TypePad's "backstage" leads you step-by-step through the rest of the process. You'll choose a template, add a personal profile stating a bit about yourself, create an "email me" link, and create TypeLists for your links.

The template includes a Theme, Layout, and Content. You can build your own theme if you want to, choosing the colors, typeface, and so on; or you can pick from a wide range of "one-click" themes provided by TypePad. (You'll see that the theme of this book's blog is a one-click theme.)

The next step is Layout. How do you want the material to appear on the screen? Experiment and see which layouts work for you. (More on this in a moment.)

Finally, in Content, you decide where the components will go. For example, you can add a Google Search function, which will find specific terms anywhere in your blog. (After a few months of steady posting, you'll be grateful for it!) You can also add functions like a link to your profile, Archives, Recent Posts, Recent Comments, and so on. You can drag these functions around and see how they look. More importantly, you'll see exactly how accessible each feature is in particular locations.

Creating TypeLists could be the next step, or you may want to wait until you're more familiar with the online resources you want to use. In any case, you will certainly want to create a "QuickPost" function. TypePad tells you how to do it; it's basically a matter of clicking a button onscreen, and then dragging the QuickPost up into the toolbar of your browser. The latest Typepad update calls this function "Blog It."

QuickPost is so handy that you'll wonder how you ever did without it. When you're on a website that you want to add to a TypeList, just click on QuickPost. A window pops open, with a link to the page you're on. At the top are four tabs: Weblog, Links, Books, and Albums. The window opens on Weblogs. You can then create a post, writing text around the link, and publish it on your blog. You'll see that you can also format the text of your post.

Alternatively, you can click on the Links tab, where you can open the "Select a list" menu and assign the web page to an existing list — or create a new list for it. In the "Link title" window, you can either leave the existing name of the page, or rename it. Click on "Save Item" at the bottom of the window, and the link appears on your blog. (You can organize such links in various ways, but that doesn't concern us here.)

The Books and Albums tabs let you create lists of titles that will take you or your readers to their sites on Amazon.com. You can even display an image of the cover. If you make arrangements with

Amazon.com, you can make a small commission every time someone clicks through to a title and then buys it.

Once you have some TypeLists installed on your site, you'll find yourself adding to them constantly. You can also add research links to blog posts, but each post will be pushed further down the screen as you add posts. Scrolling in search of a link can be tedious and time-consuming, but TypeLists will stay wherever you put them at the top of the blog.

When you want to create a post, you can do it in two ways: go "backstage" and create it from scratch, or use QuickPost to include the link to a particular website. Note that you can also include text from that website. Just select the passage you want, and then click Quick-Post. You can then add your own text before you publish.

In the composition window, you'll see some obvious text-formatting buttons: B for boldface, I for italics, and so on. But notice that you can also upload a document or graphic. Click on the icon, search your hard drive for the item, and select it. This is convenient in many ways. For example, you may want to upload a word-processed file that visitors can download. Or you may have a photograph that helps explain what you're describing.

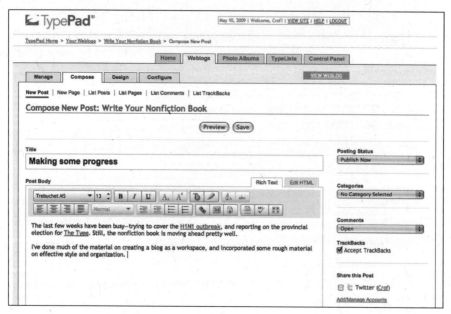

You'll also see a chain icon, which lets you create links within your post. Copy the URL from a website, select a word or phrase in your post, and click on the chain icon. Another window pops up: Paste the URL into it, click the "Ok" button, and there's an instant hyperlink in your post.

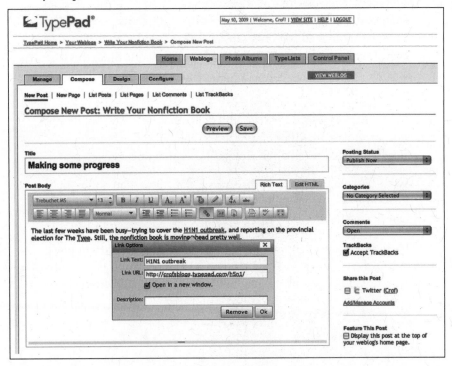

Once you've published a post, you can see how it looks on the blog. That's when the typing errors show up! But it's very easy to go back to the composition window and correct them.

## Some tips for improving blog usefulness

Usefulness is critical for a workspace blog: It needs to be useful to you, and to your readers. Out of my own experience with blogging and writing books with blogs, here are some suggestions:

1. Use a two- or three-column layout. Text that runs clear across the computer screen is really hard to read. With a three-column layout, the main column will display text in lines of 10 to 12 words. That makes text much easier to read.

2. Use dark text on a white or pale background. Pale text on a dark background is suitable for banners (where your blog title goes) and sometimes for headlines. But it's really hard to read extended passages in white-on-black.

3. Choose a readable font at a readable point size — probably no smaller than 12 points and no bigger than 16 points. Most people find text more readable on a screen if it's a "serif" font like Times New Roman, but sans serif (like Arial) can also work. Since this blog is your workspace, it should certainly be readable for you (and any online collaborators).

4. Avoid excessive use of boldface and italics. For headings, boldface is fine. Italics are good for emphasizing particular words or phrases. But long passages of boldface or italics become unreadable.

5. Keep paragraphs short — in general, not more than six or eight lines. Put a blank line between paragraphs. This gives readers a rest before moving on to the next paragraph.

Once your blog is up and running, you'll find it a convenient place to check sources while you write. If you have collaborators on your book project, you may even find it convenient to upload drafts of chapters, so everyone can read and comment on them.

# 9

# Organizing Persuasive Writing

Almost all nonfiction depends on making an *argument* that readers will believe. You can't just tell your readers, "Those are the facts; take them or leave them." You need to marshal those facts, so that readers understand them and can see the conclusions to which the facts lead. (Readers may still not buy all your arguments, but they can at least see your point.)

Like any essay or article, writing to persuade depends on gaining readers' attention, then interest, and in providing some kind of reward as the outcome. In an article, it's the kicker or zinger in the last sentence or two. In persuasive writing, the outcome is some kind of desired action by the reader: to accept the argument, to buy the house or car, or to vote for the candidate. Let's look at these three stages of persuasion: attention, interest, and action.

## Attention

In an article, you try to start with a hook that will grab your readers' attention at once. This is equally true of a nonfiction book, both for individual chapters and for the book as a whole. Consider these points as ways to gain attention:

- Show you understand your readers' concerns. This is often a matter of identifying a problem that readers recognize as such. It also helps if you "speak their language" — that is, you use a vocabulary and register that readers are comfortable with. If you're talking about grimly serious issues, a folksy tone will put readers off. But writing clearly and plainly about a technical subject, without jargon, can gain readers' gratitude and respect.

- Offer something they will agree with — perhaps a general statement, perhaps a particular observation that will help establish the foundation of your argument.

- Show what's at stake: Readers' financial security, the long-term interests of your country, or the critical importance of your great-grandmother's intelligence and character in the early history of your community. Even if the readers know what's going to happen later in the book, they want to believe it's worth their time and attention. They also want to be surprised: "I had no idea!"

- Suggest a benefit. Having established that a problem exists that deserves book-length discussion and some kind of action by the readers, you now offer a solution that readers should be willing to consider and (you hope) accept.

# Interest

Your subject already interests you enough to make you want to write a book about it. Now the job is to make your interest contagious:

- Surprise your readers with a new fact or unexpected angle on what they already know. A surprise creates a whole new perspective on what they thought they knew, and makes them more open to persuasion.

- Explain the problem or benefit in detail: a full description including facts and figures. This is very much like the expository part of an essay.

- Discuss objections calmly, then rebut them and focus on more positive arguments. Readers may be ahead of you in imagining objections, so if you raise those objections yourself and deal with them, readers at least give you credit for balance and fairness. Ignoring the opposing arguments implies that you don't want to — or can't — answer those arguments.

# Action

Maybe the only action you want from your readers is to agree that your great-grandmother was a remarkable woman. But much nonfiction really does call for some kind of action on the reader's part. Many readers may come to your book precisely because they hope you'll show them what they should do and how they should do it. You should:

- Show how action can solve the problem you've described. You may give examples of earlier actions that led to the desired outcome, or unhappy results based on failure to act.

- Make the desired action clear and easy. Phrase appeals positively: "It's not hard to help" is negative; "It's easy to help" is positive. As soon as the action gets complicated, readers will grow hesitant.

- Stress benefits of acting quickly. Set a deadline if appropriate.

- Close with a reminder of the major benefit offered.

Emotions often run high on controversial issues, and facts may be scarce. The persuasive writer must therefore be careful to rely on legitimate appeals in framing an argument, and to avoid unfairly manipulating the reader's emotions or asserting more than the evidence will allow.

## Legitimate appeals

The Greeks and Romans loved argument and debate, and we still accept their terms and rules. They also knew how to twist the terms and break the rules, and we still make bad arguments in the same ways that they did. Let's take a quick look at the basic types of legitimate appeals:

- *Logos*: appeal to logical deduction or extrapolation from established facts. This is a way of predicting what we don't yet know from direct experience.

- *Ethos*: appeal to recognized authority — people or institutions generally recognized as sound and reliable in their fields of expertise.

- *Pathos*: appeal to readers' emotions, but only combined with other legitimate appeals.

- *Experience*: appeal to scientific experiment and observation, producing results that others can duplicate, or to some kind of experience that we can assume is trustworthy.

Suppose you're writing a book on the wisdom of buying a new house. You might use all four of these appeals: With *logos*, you can predict the total cost of the house at a given interest rate for a given mortgage. Unless you make a mathematical error, readers can't disagree. With *ethos*, you cite accepted experts whose opinions agree with yours. (And if they don't agree with you, cite them anyway and show why they're wrong.) By describing cases where people failed to buy at the right time, you appeal through *pathos* to your readers' emotions: fear and pity. And finally, you might talk about your own *experience*, which makes you a kind of authority also.

## Dubious appeals

Legitimate appeals can be twisted into dubious appeals. In some cases the distortion may still lead to a valid conclusion, but it's far from persuasive:

- *Logos* can turn into nonsense if the premises of a logical argument are doubtful or the conclusion doesn't follow from them (UFOs exist, so we're under observation by a superior civilization from another planet).

- *Ethos* can turn into citing celebrities (Hollywood stars support Barack Obama!) or into citing of authorities outside their field of expertise (this astronaut doesn't believe in global warming!).

- *Pathos* can turn into emotional manipulation (strangers at the playground threatening our children!).

- *Experience* can turn into mere anecdotal evidence (My Aunt Agatha saw a UFO).

## Unacceptable appeals

We also have forms of argument that are not usually as effective, and they've been around for so long that many of them have Latin names. You should be able to avoid making these mistakes in your own arguments — and to spot those mistakes in the arguments of your opponents.

- **Ad hominem** (to the man): "That's a typical Rush Limbaugh argument." This comment attacks a person rather than the argument. "Isn't it just like a woman to say that" is also an ad hominem argument.

- **Two wrongs:** "The enemy commits atrocities, so we should also do so." However, if it's wrong for our enemies, it's wrong for us as well.

- **Common practice:** "Everyone pays women less, so we do too." Common practice once included burning those who were assumed to be witches. Common practice does not dictate ethical practice.

- **Straw man:** "My opponent wants a dictatorship." If I can't find real reasons to object to my opponent, I'll try to make people think he holds some kind of awful belief or does something objectionable, even if he doesn't.

- **False dilemma:** "Do it my way or you're doomed." Simplifies an argument by making only one position seem acceptable; all others will fail, so we may ignore them.

- **Slippery slope:** "Every hard-drug addict starts with marijuana." Premise: One step in a given direction will lead inevitably to many more steps, and the outcome will be disaster.

- **False analogy:** "Saddam Hussein was just like Hitler." For an argument by analogy to be valid, all relevant points of comparison must be valid also.

- **Special pleading:** "Yeah, I killed him, but I've got a bad temper and he made me mad." This fallacy recognizes a generally held belief (like equality or justice) but asks for an exemption in a particular case.

- **Post hoc ergo propter hoc** (after this, therefore because of this): "I lost my lucky rabbit's foot and the next day my boss fired me." The assumption is that whatever happens first is the cause of what happens next. This is not always the case.

- **Begging the question:** "If women were good bosses, we'd have more women bosses." In other words, we assume the truth of an idea we are supposed to be testing.

- **Hasty generalization:** "A Canadian swindled me once. They're all crooks." This is an extreme form of anecdotal evidence.

- **Wishful thinking:** "They'll find a cure for lung cancer before smoking kills me." This springs from our understandable desire for things to work out well, but it is an unsound argument.

- **Readers' prejudices and anxieties:** "We should ban all travel from China to prevent a pandemic." Offers a simple, thought-free, and sometimes unreasonable solution to a complex problem.

- **False authorities:** "According to Madame Blavatsky, Lemuria was a lost continent in the Indian Ocean." Madame Blavatsky, however, was no geologist, and no one should take such an authority seriously.

Where a definite conclusion seems hard to prove, bear in mind three useful principles:

- **Occam's razor:** William of Occam (or Ockham) was a medieval English scholar. He argued that, all things being equal, we should choose the simplest explanation that fits the facts. So a mysterious light in the night sky may be a flying saucer from the Galactic Empire, but first we should make sure it's not a routine commuter flight (or the planet Venus).

- **Those who assert must prove:** It is not enough for UFO believers to demand that their opponents prove UFOs don't exist; the burden of proof is on the believers to justify their assertion that UFOs do exist. This is why defendants in court plead "not guilty" instead of "innocent"; if they asserted their innocence, they might have to prove it. By contrast, those who prosecute have made an assertion — the defendant has committed an offence — and must therefore prove it.

- **Strong claims demand strong evidence:** The more unlikely a claim, the more persuasive the evidence must be. This is especially true when an assertion contradicts known facts. If UFOs do indeed come from a star, and can travel faster than light, then we will have to dismantle most of what we think we know about the laws of physics. Before we go to that much trouble, we have a right to see powerful evidence for faster-than-light travel.

# Documenting Your Sources

Inevitably, you're going to be using information that doesn't come out of your memory and opinion. To persuade others, you will have to choose reliable authorities, thereby making yourself a reliable authority too.

You will waste all the energy you put into writing your book if your readers don't believe you. Everything hinges on your credibility, and your credibility in turn hinges on how well you use your sources. In any book based, at least in part, on other people's findings, you must show what is your own work and what belongs to your sources. Otherwise you run the risk of plagiarism, or at least of undermining your credibility.

What's more, your own work should be more than just an occasional sentence that stitches one quotation to another. You are using your sources to make your points — not just to be a mouthpiece for your sources. Keep in mind the following suggestions.

## Decide what's common knowledge in the field

As a general rule, the same basic fact found in three different sources (especially without being footnoted in those sources) is *common knowledge* and you do not have to cite it. However, you may find that citing the fact as it appears in one of your sources can lend extra authority to your assertions.

If you find that all your sources agree on some point, then you can say: "All authorities agree that SARS emerged in southern China late in 2002." You don't have to footnote such a general statement. But you would be wise to document your generalization with a quote from one of those authorities, and then to footnote that quotation.

Or, if you find that three authorities think that SARS is gone for good, and two others think it's going to come back, you can say: "Authorities disagree on whether SARS is a permanent problem." You can then cite one or two sources on each side.

## Understand the perils of plagiarism

Plagiarism is a type of theft of intellectual property; copying someone's writing closely or word for word. The word comes from the Latin *plagiarius*, meaning a kidnapper. Some students are notoriously willing to plagiarize, especially when it looks like an easy way to get through a course they don't care about anyway.

But in the business world, plagiarism means lawsuits and big money. Consider the case of Sarah McLachlan, whose former colleague sued the singer because he believed she used words and a melody from a song he wrote. Comedian Eddie Murphy paid a large settlement to a screenwriter who proved Murphy had copied the writer's script for one of his movies. And a young *New York Times* reporter resigned after it was proven that he had plagiarized many of his stories while making up the rest.

The contract you sign with your publisher will almost certainly contain a clause in which you promise that your manuscript contains nothing plagiarized. That's because your publisher doesn't want to get sued.

Apart from being dishonest, plagiarism is increasingly easy to trace. An editor can simply type a key phrase into a search engine, and the original source will pop up in a second or less.

It's not enough just to paraphrase the information you find. You can put your source's facts and ideas into your own words, but they still belong to the source.

Don't worry too much. The purpose of citation is to show your readers where to find your sources, and to make sure you're quoting them accurately and in context. For scholarly work, this can be very detailed. For books intended for a general audience, citation can be much simpler, as long as interested readers can still find your sources. We'll get into the details in the next few pages.

## Offer your own opinions, and back them up

Don't treat a source with automatic respect. Any idiot can get into print, and lots do. You'll do your book and your readers a great service simply by not taking your sources as unquestionably true. You're their judge. They will have to prove to you that they're right, and then you can endorse them or repudiate them.

Don't simply say, "I agree with Smith," or "I think Smith is wrong." Appeal to your other sources, or to logic. Show how other authorities agree with Smith as well, or how they disagree. Or by applying logic to a source's argument, you could say:

"If Smith were right about the doubling rate of swine flu, everyone on earth would be infected by next January. According to recent figures from the World Health Organization, the doubling rate has fallen dramatically. Therefore, Smith is wrong."

## Use transitional phrases to smooth the reader's path

Earlier, I discussed parataxis and hypotaxis: The first relies on the reader making the jump between two seemingly unrelated ideas, while the second leads the reader carefully from one idea to the next. While parataxis can be very powerful, it works poorly if you're mixing your own ideas with those of your sources.

So you will confuse your readers by jumping from your own comments to quotations without preparing them for the change. Consider the two following passages:

- "Flame wars" — abusive exchanges — are a hazard of joining debates in Internet newsgroups. "Combatants use language ranging from the crude to the libelous." Other participants enjoy the no-holds-barred disputes. "Flame wars are an acceptable price to pay for freedom of speech."

- "Flame wars" — abusive exchanges — are a hazard of joining debates in Internet newsgroups. According to Sarah Chang, "Combatants use language ranging from the crude to the libelous." Other participants enjoy the no-holds-barred disputes. In the words of one veteran debater, Joe Jones, "Flame wars are an acceptable price to pay for freedom of speech."

I think you'll agree that the second version makes more sense, because the introductory phrases make the quotations more understandable.

## Blend quotations into your own work

A challenging aspect of documentation is using it effectively to make your points accurately and smoothly, without plagiarizing.

Suppose the following passage was something you wanted to use in your book. You might help or hurt your argument depending on how you use it:

> Despite the poor fit between school and work, benefits to graduates are certainly real, and they do make life pleasanter. But they're not what they used to be; median earnings of university graduates decreased between 1986 and 1997.
>
> According to the 2001 census, Vancouver residents with just high-school graduation earned an average of $27,000 in that year. Meanwhile those with a college certificate or diploma earned $35,388; those with a trades certificate or diploma earned $35,418. And those with a university certificate, diploma, or degree earned an average of $46,016.

1. A plagiarism of the source:

> In 2001, average income was $27,000 for Vancouverites with only high school graduation. Meanwhile, those with a college certificate or diploma earned $35,388.

The first sentence is an unacknowledged paraphrase; the second is a straight word-for-word copy. Both are plagiarisms. A serious reader will instantly wonder where you got your facts, and why you didn't mention your sources. Your credibility suffers just by writing such a paragraph.

2. A clumsy use of the source:

> The more education, the higher the income, says Crawford Kilian. "Benefits to graduates are certainly real." It's especially helpful to have a university degree. "And those with a university certificate, diploma, or degree earned an average of $46,016."

The quotations don't blend clearly with the writer's own text. Readers will feel confused by this patchwork.

3. A more effective use of the source:

One writer on education asserts that college and university graduates benefit from higher education. Crawford Kilian, citing Canada Census figures, says that Vancouver residents with only high-school graduation earned an average of $27,000 in 2001. "Meanwhile," he adds, "those with a college certificate or diploma earned $35,388; those with a trades certificate or diploma earned $35,418. And those with a university certificate, diploma, or degree earned an average of $46,016."

## Cite your sources

These passages use a very basic citation style: the name of the author, and nothing else. Readers will have to look at the back of your book to find "Crawford Kilian" in your bibliography, where they can find the original article cited like this:

Kilian, Crawford. "Today's Degree: Buyer Beware." *The Tyee.* February 5, 2004. http://www.thetyee.ca/Views/current/Todays+Degree+Buyer+ Beware.htm.

Depending on the kind of book you're writing and the audience you're writing for, you can cite your sources in any of several ways.

## For general readers

These are people who just want some general information about your subject. They're not experts or scholars, though some might enjoy exploring your sources. In such cases, a reference to the source in your text and a bibliographic notation at the end of the book should be sufficient.

For example, in my book on the black pioneers of British Columbia, I began with an anecdote about a racist prank that turned violent in the San Francisco of the gold rush. I alluded to my source:

[Mifflin] Gibbs could recall the incident half a century later in his auto-biography, *Shadow and Light* ...

And I then listed that book in the bibliography:

Gibbs, Mifflin Wistar. *Shadow and Light: An Autobiography.* Washington, D.C., 1901. Facsimile edition published in New York: Arno Press and *The New York Times*, 1968.

This is a fairly standard format for listing a book: Author's last name, first name. *Title in italics.* Place of publication: publisher and date. (Gibbs self-published the first edition; no publisher is listed for it.) You might also consider following a specific style guide, such as the *Chicago Manual of Style.*

## For specialist readers

For a more scholarly audience, you should provide a more detailed form of citation. Here it can become complicated, but it's not impossible. And if you can master the appropriate citation style, your editors will be very grateful.

The two most common styles of academic citation are usually known as MLA (Modern Languages Association) and APA (American Psychological Association). MLA is the usual format for studies in fields such as literature and languages. APA covers social and behavioral sciences. In engineering and other technical fields, IEEE (Institute of Electrical and Electronics Engineers) style is preferred. And many science subjects rely on the style used by *Science* magazine. (You'll find links to the relevant styles in this book's blog at http://crofsblogs.typepad.com/nonfiction.)

In many cases, your potential publishers will specify the citation style they expect in submitted manuscripts. You should plan to follow those specifications very closely, for a simple reason: The less work you create for your editors, the more likely you are to publish your book.

## Create your own style guide

One part of an editor's work is creating a style guide or sheet for a specific book: For example, the English spelling of Chinese terms and names can be Wade-Giles (Mao Tse-Tung) or pinyin (Mao Zedong). Canadians write "cheques," while Americans write "checks"; which spelling should you follow?

Such a style guide can help you remember to spell such words consistently, thereby saving your editor a lot of trouble and making you a low-maintenance writer.

So I suggest you build your own style guide to ensure consistency of spelling, capitalization, and other usages. If your intended publisher already has such a guide, follow it closely. And if your editor wants you to change your style, do so unless you have very serious reasons to dig in your heels.

You will save yourself countless hours of work if you start with a style guide that you consult from the first page, and if you keep a regular record of the sources you mention. It's much harder if you have to go back over the whole manuscript to impose some consistency on it.

# Interviewing Techniques

## Face-to-face

Sometimes you will simply lack the time to do face-to-face interviews as part of your research. But if time permits and such interviews are critical to the success of your book, make sure that you get the most out of them. A good interview is a well-planned interview.

1. Do your homework: research the topic and the "source" — the person you're going to interview.

2. Create a theme that your interview will illustrate. A major purpose of the interview will be to obtain quotes, anecdotes and other evidence to support that theme. (But be prepared for the unexpected!)

3. List question topics in advance — as many as you can think of. Guess what answers you may get; this will suggest still more questions. Better to think of them before the interview than after.

4. Write a letter asking for permission to conduct the interview. Suggest a time limit (30 minutes, two hours, whatever seems reasonable) and suggest a date.

5. Think about how the source will react to this interview, and develop a plan that will acknowledge the source's attitude as well as your requirements.

6. When you arrive at the interview, make sure the source is comfortable and relaxed. This may require putting the source in a familiar place, and making it clear that the source, not you, is in charge of the interview.

7. Note details: the source's physical appearance, clothing, manner, tone of voice, gestures, surroundings. These may not end up in the book, but they will help you put the source's comments in context.

8. Ensure that the source understands who you are and what the purpose of the interview is.

9. Make it clear you will use this material, especially if the source isn't used to being interviewed.

10. Ask short questions and give enough time for an answer.

11. Ask the source to repeat or clarify complex or vague answers.

12. Read back answers if asked to, or when in doubt about the phrasing of crucial material.

13. Avoid lecturing, debating, or arguing with the source.

14. Respect your source's requests for non-attribution, backgrounder-only, or off-the-record if the source makes this the condition of the interview or of a statement. But, be ready to say the interview won't happen if the limits are too strict.

15. Prefer open questions to closed ones. A closed question would be: "Where did you go to college?" An open question: "What was the most rewarding aspect of your college education?"

16. Consider different types of questions:

- Hypothetical: "What if they fired you?"

- Leading: "Don't you think he was biased in that decision?"

- Intentional Distortion: "Isn't it true you've called for higher taxes?" (Works well if the source isn't afraid of disagreeing with you, doesn't worry about pleasing you, and is interested in the topic).

- Reflective Probe: "Well, that was a mistake." "You think he was wrong?"

- Echo: "Well, that was a mistake." "A mistake?"

- Treading Water: "Well, that was a mistake." "Why is that?"

17. Afterward, send a thank-you note.

Many professional journalists rely on their recorders and their own memories to ensure that they quote their sources accurately. But in many cases, it's a good idea to ask your source to review what you've written about the interview. You may find that you completely misunderstood some critical point, and the source's response will save you both embarrassment and work.

You will also find that when you give your source a chance to check what you've written, the source will be glad to do another interview.

## Email interviews

In many cases, you will have to use email to reach your sources. Email is certainly convenient, but it also has some hazards and drawbacks. To get the most out of such interviews, bear in mind some basic qualities of email.

To begin with, format is much less important. While email systems vary, most tend to produce an address block resembling an inter-office memorandum. The "From" line contains the sender's name and email address, the "To" line has the recipient's name and email address, and the "Subject" line suggests the main topic of the message. The address block may also include "carbon copies" going to other persons or groups:

> From: Foster Goodwill, fgoodwill@intergate.ca
>
> To: Herb Linguini, hlinguini@customsoft.ca
>
> Subject: Interview topics
>
> cc: bjones@customsoft.ca

Because some people receive dozens of emails every day, they appreciate a subject line that indicates how much priority the message deserves:

> URGENT: Questionnaires needed by Friday
>
> JOKE: Bill Gates goes to Heaven

Obviously, the second message can wait.

The message itself is usually much less formal in appearance than a standard business letter. For example, it often lacks a "Dear Herb" salutation; the writer may settle for:

> Herb —

or

> Hi, Herb!

— or nothing at all. For a first email to a person you don't know, however, it's often wise to fall back on formality:

> Dear Mr. Linguini,

If Mr. Linguini replies and signs his email as "Herb," you can assume you're now on a first-name basis. If the signature is "Herbert Linguini," you should continue to address him as "Mr. Linguini."

The body of the message should include any necessary background, the information that you're providing, and some kind of action statement: "Please let me know by Sunday if you can answer my questions," or "I'll insert your corrections in my text as soon as I receive them."

Background is important. Imagine yourself firing off email messages all morning to several sources. After lunch you get a reply from one of them: "I completely agree."

Agree with what? Until you go back to check your original message, you may have no idea what this agreement is about. Your correspondent has made your job harder than it has to be.

Another hazard is to include the whole text of the other person's message, which may be very long, only to add: "I completely agree."

A better approach is to summarize the other person's message (orientation) and then comment on it (information and action):

> Hi, Foster,
>
> Thanks for your note about rescheduling Monday's phone interview. Wednesday, November 2 would work very well. That will give me more time to review what you've sent me already. I look forward to talking with you.
>
> Best wishes,
>
> Herb Linguini
>
> hlinguini@pesto.ca

You can also copy just a short, relevant excerpt from the previous message:

Hi, Foster — you wrote:

> Would it be possible to reschedule our Monday phone interview? I've just realized that I'll be flying home from Seattle that day.

The message still requires a complimentary close (Best wishes or Cheers or Regards), a signature, and the writer's email address. These are not absolutely essential, but your message may seem brusque without them.

## Effective email is courteous email

When you write email, you should also understand the limitations of the computer monitor. Its resolution isn't very good compared to print on paper, and the screen itself may be too bright or dim for comfortable reading.

As a result, when you read from a monitor, your reading speed drops by as much as 30 percent. Furthermore, proofreading becomes harder, especially in a long message. Many messages are a solid block of text on the screen, without gaps between paragraphs; this discourages careful reading.

Keep your email messages as short and clear as possible. Break up text into short paragraphs (usually not more than five or six lines), with white space between them. This will make your reader's job easier. You will also find it easier to proofread your message before sending it.

If you are sending a detailed questionnaire, format the email to make answers easy. (If your source has a compatible word processor, you may even send the questionnaire as an attached word-processor file, which the source can add to.)

Some computer users think the value of email lies in its speed: you just type a note and send it without worrying about spelling or grammar. Errors in replies, too, can be overlooked. This is not so. Much depends on your sources' good will, and if your email conveys sloppiness, it also conveys disrespect. Your sources are doing you a favor, and you should make it as easy as possible to do so.

Proofreading is hard to do on a computer screen, but it's worth the effort. A typo or punctuation error could change the whole meaning of the message. Consider the implication of the hyphen in the following:

- I resent your questions

- I re-sent your questions

None of this matters when you're writing to old high-school friends, but for interviewees it definitely matters.

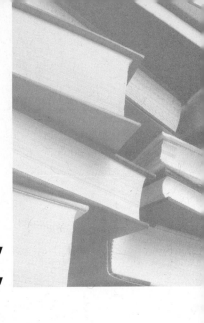

# PART 3:
# WRITING

# 10

# Starting the Writing Process

Planning, researching, writing, and marketing usually overlap. Your research findings affect your planning, and planning may involve writing articles that help create a market. The articles may then turn up in the book.

Still, it's easier to deal with each of these stages separately, and now we're going to deal with what happens when you stare into the screen and start putting words on it.

## Basic Nonfiction Storytelling Devices

The article-writing techniques discussed in Chapter 4 are entirely applicable when writing book chapters. You could even say that "Hey-You-See-So-Ha!" applies on every level of writing, from each paragraph to each chapter to the entire book.

Readers love a story, and the same techniques that fiction writers use are also at your disposal. The only difference is that in your book, the techniques deal with matters of fact. Here are some suggestions on storytelling techniques and how to apply them in nonfiction.

## In medias res

This is Latin for "in the middle of things." Homer used it in *The Iliad*, so it's not exactly avant-garde. This device exploits the storyteller's need to grab the reader's attention with something unusual or dramatic, and to start the story in the midst of the events covered in the books — ideally, with an incident that makes the conclusion inevitable.

Suppose you're writing a family history, and you decided to embark on the project after attending your grandmother's funeral and then listening to your mother reminisce about her parents. The funeral and that conversation are the natural starting point for your book.

What's more, your mother has told you enough to make you realize how little you really know about your own family, so the book will hopefully tell you and your relatives a lot about the family.

An element of mystery, and the promise of solving that mystery, is a basic part of storytelling. In *Citizen Kane*, we see the dying newspaper baron mutter "Rosebud," and the rest of the movie is a search to find out what he meant.

In fiction, writers often start with their main characters under some kind of serious stress, and the rest of the story shows how they deal with that stress.

I used that version of *in medias res* on the first page of my book *Go Do Some Great Thing: The Black Pioneers of British Columbia*. I had an anecdote about two black merchants in gold-rush San Francisco. They suffered a stupid and violent practical joke that dramatized the problems faced by black Americans in the 1850s. Those problems in turn led San Francisco's blacks (including the merchants) to emigrate to British Columbia in search of freedom. The rest of the book is about what they experienced there, and what they did about it.

I could have begun the book much earlier, perhaps with the birth of one of the merchants, or a little later with the arrival of the blacks in Victoria in April 1858. But the practical joke — which involved the beating of one of the merchants — was dramatic, and gave me an opportunity to explain the predicament of San Francisco's black community in the 1850s. The predicament motivated their departure, and motivation is critical to any story.

## The scene

In fiction, the basic unit is the scene: a passage in which the characters involved face a challenge, try to overcome the challenge, and succeed or fail.

In the process, readers learn something important about the characters' personalities, talents, and moral qualities, and about the situation they're in. Readers are also prepared for major revelations later in the story, when the characters face their climactic struggle.

In nonfiction, every anecdote is a kind of scene. In a family history, the story about Aunt Mary and the Christmas turkey tells us something about Aunt Mary and about the family. In a how-to book on sailing Lake Superior, anecdotes about places, people, and problems will enliven the book and give weight to the points you're making. "Anecdotal evidence" isn't very acceptable in science, but we tend to believe the anecdotes that come out of our own lives.

You don't want to make your book into a random collection of family gossip, but where an anecdote really illustrates something important to your theme, it's invaluable. As with anecdotes used in articles, such mini-stories tend to hold reader interest, and the punch line gives them a quick reward for their attention. That makes them keep reading to find the next reward.

## Plot

Fiction has plots. Real life just has one thing after another. Still, the basic technique of plotting can make some kinds of nonfiction much more readable. This is especially true for genres like the memoir and the history, where emphasis falls on an individual's personality and motivation: Someone does something, whether out of grim determination or a casual whim, and important consequences result.

The basic plot comes from the Bible: We start in paradise, something goes wrong, and we're cast out into a harsh world where we have to struggle to survive. If we learn our lesson and persevere, we may get back to some form of paradise — either the rural happiness of the Garden of Eden, or the urban joys of heaven where the streets are paved with gold.

In a family memoir, the expulsion from Eden might be an ancestor's major setback: I know I'm here because my great-grandfather Heinrich Kilian went bankrupt in 1880s Germany, and migrated with his family to America. If he hadn't, my grandfather would never have met my grandmother Daisy Johnston.

In fiction, the struggle of the main characters requires some kind of insecurity that motivates them to regain a stable and secure life. They gain that life (or fail to gain it) thanks to a mix of circumstances and personal character. The fiction writer creates scenes that dramatize those circumstances and character traits.

In nonfiction, the writer has to find documented events that do the same with real people. This is not as hard as it sounds. If you're writing a history of your city, you may discover that the first mayor was a drunk and a bigamist. This is great gossip, but it also suggests aspects of his character that explain his politics or the temper of his times. His drinking led him to oppose the local prohibitionists; his bigamy reflected a culture when it was easier to desert a spouse than to divorce.

As you learn more about the people and times that you're writing about, you'll draw conclusions that you want to persuade your readers to accept — for example, that Mayor Smith may have been a drunk and a bigamist, but he deeply believed in the future of his city and worked hard to make it prosper.

To persuade your readers, you'll pick the incidents and anecdotes that help to make your case. In the process, you're creating the nonfiction version of a plot. But to make a really solid case, you can't just ignore the incidents and anecdotes that undercut your case. Honesty and fairness require you to bring in that evidence as well, and to deal with it. Maybe the mayor won't be as clear-cut a person as you'd like him to be, but your readers will be glad to have all the evidence and to make up their own minds about him.

## Showing and telling

Nonfiction relies heavily on exposition: The author telling the reader one thing after another. But readers are more likely to believe you if you show them — that is, put them into a situation where they draw their own conclusions.

For example, in my book about BC's black pioneers, I found an incident involving a black man named John Freemont Smith, who served as an Indian agent for the Canadian government early in the twentieth century. He got into a conflict with a white officer, Lt.-Col. Flick, who refused to work with Smith simply because he was black.

I didn't need to tell readers that the officer was a racist bigot; I just had to quote from a letter he wrote to the government:

"The Canadian Militia is a military organization of whitemen who represent the Anglo-Saxon race, and men of colour have nothing to do with our deliberations. ... We, in the west, have an idea that races subject to the whiteman are better when governed by a whiteman."

And that's just the nice part of what he said! So readers could decide for themselves about Lt.-Col. Flick, judging him by his own words, not mine.

## Dialogue

For some reason, people love to read anything in quotation marks. In fiction, dialogue can disguise exposition, reveal character, and move the plot along. It can do the same in nonfiction.

In some cases, the dialogue is there in your published sources: This is what the governor was quoted as saying during the hearings, and this is what his or her attorney said to the media afterward. In other cases, your interviewees and sources will give you "monologues" that work just as well: your Dutch grandmother's memories of arriving in Canada after World War II, or an engineer's description of building a levee protecting your town from a flood-prone river.

In such cases you may record your sources word-for-word, and just transcribe what they tell you. But you may also find that if you listen attentively, you can re-create what they tell you. It won't be as rambling or repetitious as their original statements, but if you let them read your version, they're likely to say, "That's exactly what I said!" Whichever way you choose, readers will love hearing your sources speak.

## Suspense

Uncertainty creates suspense, and readers keep turning the pages until the suspense is resolved. The uncertainty may be about the fate of the people you're discussing in your family memoir, or about what's going to be in the next chapter of your self-help book. Even if we know, in general, what's going to happen, we're uncertain about the details — and we keep reading to learn them.

So if you start a chapter with, "On the day my grandfather died, he had ham and eggs for breakfast," we will keep reading out of morbid fascination. In your book on yoga techniques, a throwaway line like, "This approach, as we will see, leads to dramatic improvement — but it may also lead to serious injury," will ensure continued interest.

The reward for such interest should be a powerful jolt of new understanding, making your reader think: "I never knew *that* before!" or "So *that's* what really happened!" To make sure readers have such a response, the new knowledge should be truly surprising and important, and not quite predictable.

Suspense is guaranteed if you make it clear that the stakes are very high, for the characters or for the readers themselves: a successful career or a tragic death could be the outcome.

## Characterization

Novelists build fictitious characters out of endless factual details: what they wear, whether they prefer tennis or golf, their allergies to the cats they can't live without, their sense of humor (or lack of it). If you're writing about people you know, or about well-documented persons, your job is fairly easy: You have a wealth of anecdotes and details that will bring your characters to life.

In other cases, you may have very little to go on: a photograph, perhaps, and a few biographical details. In such cases, it's wise to stick to what you know for sure, instead of speculating about traits the person may or may not have had.

In any case, a couple of important details may be powerfully evocative, giving readers a better sense of the person than if we had a whole dossier on his or her life.

In still other cases, we can leave the characterization to the character: A quote from Ralph Waldo Emerson might tell us more about him as a person than a five-page biography would.

## Climax

In fiction, the climax is the final showdown between the protagonist and whoever or whatever the opponent is: a blizzard, Darth Vader, or the woman competing for the heroine's boyfriend. Everything that's come before the climax has been preparation, showing us the resources that the adversaries will bring to the confrontation.

In nonfiction, a climax may be harder to offer your readers. Maybe it will be the death of your grandmother, offering a chance to assess all the achievements of her life. Or it might be the outcome of an election that ended a long era of corruption thanks to a resourceful and honest mayoral candidate.

A nonfiction book is essentially a long argument, and the climax can be the final bit of evidence that clinches your case. A statement by an unquestioned authority, the latest research study, or even some fact that you began with is even more effective when you return to it.

In a sense, all fiction and nonfiction genres are arguments. The novelist tells a story that entertains while arguing a particular vision of the world. So does the nonfiction writer. Even a how-to book like this one argues that writing nonfiction is a craft that anyone can master, given enough determination.

Fiction and nonfiction alike present a body of information that turns into *exformation*: The readers know it, generally accept it, and keep reading with that exformation in mind. The climax reminds them of some scrap of exformation that they may not have even thought about since reading it on page 17. Making that connection will give them a paratactic jolt — like hearing an old lover's voice, or learning via Google that an old friend died years ago.

This principle applies even in nonfiction books that don't seem to have much of a story. An academic textbook, for example, ordinarily starts with basic principles and encourages students to apply those principles in various exercises or problems. It then relies on an understanding of the principles as students tackle more complex and subtle points. Ideally, they should feel a jolt as they make the connection between exformation (knowledge already absorbed) and information (new material).

Such a jolt is hard to argue with. It knocks down our defenses, and we want it to. "Anticlimax," after all, is a word for disappointment, for a letdown. Whatever your subject, your readers would rather be overwhelmed than left dangling.

# 11

## Some Basic Writing Elements

If you are writing nonfiction early in the twenty-first century using on-line resources, you are writing for a different audience than has anyone before you.

The first writing systems — hieroglyphics, cuneiform, Chinese and Mayan ideograms — were highly specialized and open to only a tiny minority. Literacy was like modern quantum physics — a powerful tool almost no one knew how to use.

Today we have billions of people who are literate in print, and almost as many who are also literate in online media that include text on a computer screen. But the new media have changed our reading habits, as I discovered to my surprise when I began to rewrite my book on the black pioneers.

My first step was to create a computer file of the manuscript. Since the book had been published long before I started writing on computers, this meant transcribing the text from a copy of the first edition.

The sheer length of my paragraphs amazed me. How could I have gone on and on in one paragraph, filling most of a page before starting a new paragraph? And how could the sentences in those paragraphs be so long? I'd known for years that text designed to be read on a website should be mostly short sentences in mostly short paragraphs. The difficulty of reading on a low-resolution computer screen makes it hard to plow through long stretches of text. I hadn't realized that years of writing and reading web text had broken me of my old print-on-paper reading habits.

Studying writing on the web had also taught me that readers pay the most attention to the beginnings and ends of paragraphs. They may still read the sentences in the middle, but they're not as responsive to the content. So the real impact comes from the content of the first and last sentences. The more paragraphs, the more impact.

If your book is going to appear online, bear in mind that your readers are likely to be impatient with long, complex sentences and ten-line paragraphs. And even if you're writing exclusively for print on paper, long sentences and paragraphs will affect your readability, and therefore the size of your audience.

## Readability

Various readability scales are available. They generally count the number of syllables per word, the number of words per sentence, and the number of sentences per paragraph to determine readability. It's usually defined as the number of years of formal education a reader should have to be able to understand you. If your readability is, say, grade 15, then theoretically anyone with less than three years of post-secondary education will have trouble understanding your text.

I'm not suggesting that you dumb down your writing, but if you keep it as clear and simple as possible, everyone will be grateful — even your Ph.D. readers.

Years ago, I typed a chapter of the Book of Ecclesiastes into a Word file. I cheated: Every sentence in Ecclesiastes is a separate paragraph, but I used three sentences per paragraph. Then I ran it through the simple readability tool in Word (you'll find it by using Spelling and

Grammar, in the Tools menu, or on the Review tab, depending on your version of Word).

Even with my longer paragraphs, Ecclesiastes came in at grade three readability. A primary student could understand a document that great minds have studied for over 2,000 years. If only you and I could write that well!

In this section of the book we'll look at ways to write as concisely and clearly as possible. Apart from the readability tools built into Word and other word processors, you can also check your readability at Readability.info. At this very useful site, you can either type in the URL of a website, or upload a Word document, and the site will give you a detailed critique and several different readability scores.

By the way, this Readability section of the book tests out with Word at grade 9.9 readability. That's not bad, but I'd prefer to hit grade 6.

# Structure

In discussing articles, I mentioned three ways to organize your material: narrative, by category, and by logical argument. As you begin to write your book, you'll find you need all three structural components.

For example, if you're writing a family or community history, the overall structure may be narrative, but you may be justified in making a logical argument to fill in something you can't find direct evidence for. Or, to explain some issue, you may need to shift to categorical organization for a few pages.

Even if you're writing about a very current issue like public-health policy or corporate law, where categorical organization is required, narrative structure can be useful for establishing the historical background your readers need if they're going to understand your arguments about the present.

This is also a good time to remember hypotaxis and parataxis. To write using hypotaxis means making clear connections between ideas so readers understand what's important and what's less important. It relies on transitional and subordinating words like "next," "third," "however," "when," and "although." Hypotaxis is usually the best strategy for most writers.

However (note the transitional word!), you may get more powerful results from parataxis, where the transitional words disappear and each idea stands on its own. Readers make their own connections between ideas. They connect what you've previously told them with what you're telling them now, or with what they know from other sources.

A recent history of World War II, *Human Smoke*, makes very effective use of parataxis. Beginning in the 1930s, the author presents a string of anecdotes and news clippings about events leading up the war and then during the war. The author makes little or no comment about these episodes.

Because we already know much about World War II from other sources (it's part of our exformation, so the author doesn't bother to include it), the news clippings make us respond much more directly and emotionally: Some politician in 1937 makes a statement, not knowing what will happen next. But we know, so we feel like spectators at a disaster.

This is a very sophisticated form of nonfiction storytelling, and perhaps a dangerous one. When we make the connection between what we already know and what we've just learned, our reaction will be emotional: "Aha! Now I understand!" or "Oh my God! Now I understand!" The first may be a happy response, like grasping a hard concept in a calculus textbook. The second may be a negative response of horror or disgust. Either way, our emotions may cause us to accept the author's arguments less critically. We may then trust the author more than we should.

Perhaps the wisest course for such an author would be to create the emotional impact and then invite readers to analyze their reactions. Maybe you've just told them something shocking about the early history of your community. Now you can explain why the people of that era held a particular attitude, and you can argue that we can't judge our ancestors by our present values.

# 12

# Semantics and Style

We've all heard politicians attack their opponents as merely peddling "semantics" and "rhetoric." But those terms refer to very powerful tools, and they're tools that you will use as a nonfiction writer — whether you realize it or not.

"Rhetoric" is the whole system of techniques we use in writing and speech, including figures of speech, word choice, rhythms, and structure. It comes from the Greek word *rhetor*, meaning "a public speaker." Precisely because rhetoric is so effective, it can be abused.

Semantics is a more recent term, meaning the study of the meanings of words. You could say that semantics is the theory, and rhetoric is the practice, of how we communicate with one another.

Semantics defines two kinds of meanings for words:

- Denotation: the meaning of a word without emotional associations. "Table" is a sequence of letters that denotes a particular piece of furniture or a chart of numerical values. We don't have feelings, one way or another, about such a term.

- Connotation: the emotional associations of a word. "Grandma's antique table" can express considerable emotion, at least among her grandchildren.

Connotations can change dramatically over time. "Nazi" denotes a member of the National Socialist German Workers' Party. The original Nazis chose their party's name because the words had positive connotations for Germans in the 1920s. But Nazi now connotes a whole range of ideas that most people find horrifying and repugnant: dictatorship, racism, war, and genocide.

When we use words with strong connotations, we are conveying our feelings about what we're discussing. We usually do so without even thinking about it, which is why it's easy for others to use semantics to manipulate us with words that provoke our emotions.

Such "purr words" and "snarl words" can influence readers and listeners by short-circuiting rational thought. Call someone a "terrorist" and everyone feels hostile. Call someone a "freedom fighter," and everyone feels friendly.

Consider some of the semantic effects of the following terms, which we often read or hear in news accounts of labor disputes:

| | |
|---|---|
| • company president | • union boss |
| • professional negotiator | • hired gun |
| • decent working conditions | • featherbedding |
| • union official | • labor faker |
| • management offer | • union demand |
| • outside agitator | • union organizer |
| • replacement workers | • scabs |

Political response to such terms may influence the livelihoods (and even lives) of countless people, but few will stop to think about the reality behind the terms that spark their emotions.

Some words have semantic impact because we associate them with groups that enjoy high prestige. Scientists have prestige, so scientific words can sound impressive: parameter, extrapolate, median, psephologist, contraindication. (If you don't know what those words mean, use Google's "define" function.)

Note that such words usually come from Greek or Latin, the languages of medieval scholarship. We still regard such words as "classier," or more prestigious, than their Anglo-Saxon equivalents. Here are some examples of Greek and Latin words and what they mean in Anglo-Saxon English:

| | |
|---|---|
| syntax | word order |
| manufacture | make |
| mundane | worldly |
| factory | workshop |
| mitigate | weaken, soften |
| physician | healer |

While Latin and Greek words are often the better choices, they are relatively abstract. If you hear the word bovine, do you instantly think of a cow? If you smelled smoke, would you call out, "Combustion"?

The careful writer, therefore, will usually choose an Anglo-Saxon word over a Latin or Greek one. (That does not mean, however, we should talk about the Canadian *folk* instead of the Canadian *people*, or refer to our physician as a *healer*).

You should consider the semantic impact of a particular choice of words. The first word that pops into your head isn't always the one to write down. While some cynics will deliberately set out to exploit people's emotions, an honest writer will try to avoid such manipulation.

# 13

## Writing Transparently

Your job as a nonfiction writer is to make your reader's job effortless. As a writer, therefore, you should try to develop a style that enables your reader to understand you at once, without being distracted by the way you say it. This is what we might call "transparent" writing.

A transparent style is not anonymous, but it doesn't call attention to itself. You achieve a transparent style by —

- remembering that you and your cleverness are not the subject, or avoiding anything that distracts the reader from the subject and draws attention to the style.

- As Ernest Hemingway said: "The test of a good piece of writing is how much good stuff you can cut out of it." In other words, purely decorative "fine writing" has no purpose in transparent writing.

Here are some hazards to avoid:

# Quirks of Diction

- Overuse of unusual words may make you feel clever, but it will baffle your readers. Avoid words like quotidian, cis-lunar, rebarbative, and cunctatory.

- Mistaking one word for another is all too common a problem. Flaunting is a different action from flouting; to infer and to imply are not the same.

- Needless repetition of words and phrases suggests you're not paying attention to yourself. For instance: "He went to the city of London. The city of London is a great city."

# Problems in Sentence Patterns and Rhythms

Too many short, simple sentences can make your text sound like a parody of Hemingway. For instance: "We went out. It was raining. We went in. It was dry."

Too many long, complex sentences will leave your readers confused: "Experts, indeed, were divided on whether the National Missile Defence, resurrected from the Reagan-era Star Wars project, might retain some military value in the aftermath of the collapse of the Soviet Union and the consequent reduction of tension among the nuclear nations."

Needless inversion of sentence order is also confusing. In this sentence, one could rightfully infer that a puck became firmly implanted into a book: "Into the record books went Iginla's goal."

# Clumsy Rhetorical Devices

- Avoid the awesome allure of assonance and the lulling, lilting loveliness of alliteration.

- Who needs rhetorical questions?

- Metaphors and similes are as striking (and useless) as fried shoes.

- Avoid obvious irony.

- Avoid obvious "plays on words" (and sometimes the appearance of quotation marks make them really obvious).

- Avoid lapses in tone.

- Try not to drop from high seriousness to slang. For instance: "The Crown should prosecute, to the fullest extent of the law of the land, these computer-criminal nerds."

- If you're going to be brutally explicit, stay that way. Don't waver between explicitness and tact, as demonstrated here: "After vomiting blood all night, he passed away."

- Coyness makes you look silly. Don't write "ladies of the evening" if referring to sex trade workers.

- Pomposity makes you look even worse. Don't call police officers "minions of the law."

- Avoid the use of bathos. Bathos is Greek for "abrupt fall"; it's great for stand-up comedy, but not for a real argument. It ruins this sentence: "Nuclear war would cause worldwide devastation, kill millions, wreck the whole planet's climate, and put an end to professional hockey."

# Dead Phrasing

- The beginning of a sentence is a "hot spot" where readers pay the most attention, so avoid sentences starting with dead terms like "There" and "It." In the examples that follow, I'll provide a dead phrase followed by a corrected phrase.

1. There are two problems that we must solve.

   *We must solve two problems.*

2. It is a pleasure to hear from you.

   *I'm pleased to hear from you.*

Watered-down modifiers are tolerable in conversation, but they weaken your writing. Avoid phrases like "sort of," "kind of," "pretty good," and "a little bit."

That also goes for hollow praise. Words like "nice," "interesting," "cute," and "great" don't mean very much — be more explicit.

# Clichés

Avoid clichés. These were once so fresh and original that everyone repeated them. Soon they became dull and stale. Clichés come in several forms:

- Proverbial (ounce of prevention, stitch in time)

- Slangy (uptight, chill out)

- Trendy (interface, parameters, empowerment)

- Psychobabble (meaningful, potential, heavily into)

To some extent, these style problems may be the vices of your virtues. As you acquire skill and confidence as a writer, you will want to show off: "And for my next trick, a multiple compound-complex sentence with three metaphors, a simile, and a triple axel!"

Well, it's a free country. Language is a wonderful toy, and play is one of its greatest uses, but save the show-off writing for your friends and family; your nonfiction writing should be as clear and simple as you can make it.

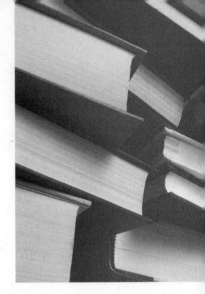

# 14

## Word Choice

Word choice is an important consideration. We recognize the power of unfamiliar words: they help to define their user as a member of a special group. Teenagers use their own slang, mountaineers have their own technical vocabulary, and bureaucrats like to sound bureaucratic. Much of this is just to send a nonverbal message: "You and I belong to the same group, unless you don't understand my dialect." Without that sense of shared language (and therefore of shared values and experience), readers are unlikely to stick with you, and even less likely to believe you.

Transparent writing, however, tries to make sure that writer and reader feel they both belong to the same group. It helps, therefore, to avoid some stylistic practices that will likely baffle your readers.

## Latinisms

To commit a Latinism is to yell "Combustion!" in a crowded theatre, when "Fire!" would have gotten your point across. The following terms aren't all easy to guess from their sound, and all have simple equivalents in plain English.

- obfuscate
- conceptualize
- meretricious
- quintessential
- utilize
- osculate

- somnambulism
- auriferous
- contraindicated
- rubicund
- defenestrate
- ubiquitous

## Greekisms

Greekisms are like Latinisms; words with Greek roots that aren't necessarily the clearest choice. Here are some examples:

- polymorphous
- hubris
- tetralogy
- oligarchy
- sinophile

- kudos
- pseudopod
- kakistocracy
- prototype
- polyandry

## Hype Words

"Hype" comes from the hypodermic needle used to inject illegal stimulants into a racehorse. Hype means a phony energy used to sell something dead. Disc jockeys and advertisers are fond of these words because they create a false atmosphere of excitement. Here are some examples:

- total
- radical
- terrific
- mega
- great
- awesome

- massive
- ultra
- hyper
- super
- tremendous
- incredible

# Vogue Words

Vogue words are like bureaucracy's slang. Bureaucrats read each other's memos and steal words and phrases that make them feel more "official." Here are some examples:

- creative
- in-depth
- prioritize
- interface
- dynamic
- input
- viable
- parameter
- bottom line
- entrepreneurial
- state of the art
- rationalize
- dysfunctional
- postmodern
- issue (in reference to a problem)
- opt
- paradigm
- synergize
- concern (in reference to a problem)
- leading edge
- cutting edge
- bleeding edge
- impact (verb)
- surface (verb)

# Euphemisms

"Euphemism" is a Greek word you should use with confidence. It means "speaking well," especially of something not very nice. (In Greek mythology the three goddesses of revenge were called "Eumenides," the kindly ones.)

Sanitized for your protection (or deception), euphemisms have relatively neutral connotations for terms that may upset us. If we don't want to think about death, violence, economic insecurity, or bodily functions, euphemisms can insulate us from reality. In other cases, a euphemism may be the only way to get your reader to think about the subject at all.

Here are some definitions followed by some fairly recent euphemisms you may have encountered:

## Economic euphemisms

**To fire an employee:** dehire, let go, outplace, declare redundant, downsize

**Poor:** economically disadvantaged

**Debts:** negative savings

**Taxes:** revenue enhancers

**Charging more than legally permitted:** over-recovery

**Used:** pre-owned

## Military/political euphemisms

**To subvert a foreign government:** destabilize

**Bomb villages, defoliate forests, or massacre peasants:** pacify

**Civilians killed accidentally in air raids:** collateral damage

**Concentration camp:** relocation centre

**Sneak attack:** pre-emptive strike

**Bombing:** air support

**Solitary confinement:** individual behavior adjustment unit

**To be shot at by allies:** friendly fire

## Aging and death euphemisms

**To poison:** put to sleep, put down

**To die:** pass away, pass on, go west, buy the farm

**Old person:** golden ager, senior citizen, 55 or better

**Handicapped:** physically or mentally challenged

**Death:** negative patient care outcome

**Eighty years old:** eighty years young

# Sleepwriting

"Sleepwriting" is the use of words in ways that make them meaningless or redundant. Some sleepwriting is caused by failure to understand what words mean. Here are some examples:

- He successfully escaped from prison. (If he didn't succeed, he didn't escape.)

- Stravinsky was the twentieth century's most perfect composer. ("Perfect" doesn't take comparatives — it's perfect or it's not.)

- Police completely surrounded the hideout. (Surrounding, by definition, is a complete action.)

- This is a totally unique home! ("Unique" doesn't take modifiers like "totally.")

- "I will be proven innocent when the true facts are revealed."

- Illiterate? Write today for free help!

Meaningless words also contribute to sleepwriting. The word "situation," for example, has become meaningless through overuse. Each of the following sentences would convey the same message even without the word "situation" entirely absent from the phrase:

- We're facing an emergency situation.

- The Middle East is in a crisis situation.

- What's today's weather situation?

Similarly, the word "exclusive" in real estate ads once meant: "Not for sale to Jews, blacks, Asians, or anyone else we don't like." Now it means nothing at all, yet it still carries a connotation of privilege that evidently appeals to some homebuyers.

Redundancy is a necessary and essential component part of sleepwriting. Some examples of redundancy:

- young juvenile
- fatal slaying
- fair and equitable

- free gift
- illegal crime
- close proximity

- each and every
- full and complete
- green colour

- end result
- added bonus
- large size

Sleepwriting is so common that we tend to "sleepread" through it, ignoring its meaninglessness. But once you've really thought about such expressions, you'll find it hard to use them again. The cure for sleepwriting is simple: write only when you're wide awake.

See Appendix 2 for a checklist for nonfiction writers and Appendix 1 for some editing exercises.

# 15

# Editing

One of my mentors, the late mystery writer Stanley Ellin, had an unusual writing technique: He wrote page one and then rewrote it as many times as needed until he was happy with it. Then he went to page two and repeated the process.

It was a slow way to write a novel or short story, but it got phenomenal results: intricate mysteries that were also brilliant social commentary.

Ellin was editing himself as he wrote, which can be a very tough way to do it unless you're a very self-confident writer with your whole book clearly mapped out.

Most writers using the Ellin method would become victims of "premature self-criticism syndrome" — the common tendency to see only mistakes in what they've written so far, with no idea how to improve.

You might think that editing is what happens after the manuscript is finished. Some books are indeed written that way. But if the publisher has to use an editor to go over your manuscript and completely revise it, production costs will rise and the book will look much less attractive.

So you'd be wise to consider editing and writing as simultaneous, each affecting the other.

Here's where your journal/blog can come in very handy. As you write, save some time to post progress reports in your journal. The important posts will be those with bad news: The book is going badly, something's not clicking, and you're feeling discouraged.

Maybe an outsider could give you some good, constructive criticism, but you yourself can be your book's best critic. If you note in your journal what's going wrong, something remarkable may happen: As you express your criticisms in simple, blunt sentences (instead of just saying, "This is awful!," you might say, "This needs more explanation"), the solutions may pop into your mind. So you write them down as well, and then apply them to the manuscript.

I have done this repeatedly with both fiction and nonfiction books, and I'm still not sure why it works. Something about the process of thinking critically, in full sentences, seems to trigger a creative response from your inner editor.

It also helps to start with a clearly defined problem in the manuscript, and then find a solution. The following guide may help.

| Problem: | Solution: |
|---|---|
| • Unclear thesis. Book's main statement or argument is vague or nonexistent. | • Try to state the book's purpose in one sentence early in the document. |
| • Poor logical development. Book uses unsupported assertions, appeals to dubious authorities, or questionable scientific findings. | • Back up assertions with appeals to recognized scientific findings, reliable authorities, and logical argument. |
| • Poor narrative development. Events are out of chronological sequence for no good reason. | • Keep events in sequence; explain when breaking sequence (for example, flashbacks). |

| | |
|---|---|
| • Poor categorical development. Links between parts are unclear or nonexistent; sequence of categories is confusing. | • Use transitional words and phrases; organize categories from least important to most important/earliest to latest, etc. |
| • Verb tense varies without good reason. | • Adopt consistent verb tense. |
| • Point of view varies without good reason. | • Adopt consistent point of view. |
| • Wordy text. | • Cut unnecessary words. |
| • Tone is unsuitably formal/informal/solemn/flippant. | • Choose words and phrases with appropriate connotations. |
| • Errors in English: spelling, grammar, punctuation. | • Consult dictionaries, style manuals, and style-checkler programs. |

## Substantive Editing

Chances are that your self-criticisms are what we call **substantive editing**: You're looking at the book's concept and how well you're putting that concept into words. Maybe you've decided to rearrange some sections because they make more sense than in your original outline. (I've done that several times with this book.) Or perhaps you've decided that some sections, even though you love them, don't really belong in the book at all.

Substantive editing requires you to develop some objectivity about your own book. Again, if you're writing letters to yourself about its progress, this objectivity is possible. You can then start improving the manuscript while it's still in progress.

For example, you can ask yourself if the manuscript is going to be understandable and interesting to its intended readers. Have you left out something important? Have you added anything your readers already know, or don't need to know?

And what about your writing style? Are you injecting yourself needlessly into the story, or maintaining an icy reserve when your own personality would enhance the story?

These are judgment calls, based on "soul search" more than research. But if you can put yourself into the shoes of your readers (including your publisher's editors), you can save everyone a lot of trouble.

## Line Editing

You may also want to consider editing the "navigation aids" of your manuscript: the table of contents, the chapter headings, subheadings within chapters, source citations, and index (both print and electronic). Are they clear and consistent?

This is part of **line editing**, when you're trying to achieve consistent usage and tone.

If you know where you're going to submit the manuscript, are you following that publisher's guidelines? If not, have you created your own style guide? (For example, if you're a Canadian, are you going to write "neighbour" or "neighbor"?) When you've introduced a person in the book, will you thereafter refer to that person by last name or first?

Line editing doesn't require judgment, but it does require you to follow rules — whether you make the rules or your publisher does.

## Copyediting

Usually the last stage in the editing process before proofreading, copyediting follows the rules of standard English usage — which are, alas, not always standard! The rules of spelling, punctuation, and grammar can vary from country to country. Even within a single country, like the US, different publishers may follow different style guides.

Still, the closer you can get to your country's version of standard English, the less work your manuscript requires from your editors. Remember that while your manuscript is a personal achievement for you, it's just another job for your editors. So the easier you make their job, the faster your book will get into print.

# Editing Tips

- Read the text out loud. Errors are often more audible than visible.

- Put the text into a font and point size you don't usually use. This will make it look "strange," like work by someone else.

- Print a draft, let it sit overnight, then edit the printout.

- Don't respect the text! Just because some words are already on the page doesn't mean they deserve to stay there. A good editor tries to look beneath the words, to find the message struggling to reach the surface.

- Don't hesitate to make changes if you can find a clearer set of words to express the message. If you need to, try writing a sentence four or five different ways and see which one gets the message across in the fewest, clearest words.

# Finding Outside Editing Help

Sometimes you realize you're just too close to your book to edit it fully, or you suspect your grammar and punctuation really aren't that strong. What now?

You may find someone among your family and friends who can do effective editing, but criticism from such sources can sometimes be hard to take. A wiser choice may be to find a freelance editor.

This is not as hard as it might seem. The Editors' Association of Canada represents hundreds of freelance editors. So does the US-based Editorial Freelancers Association. In the UK, look for the Society for Editors and Proofreaders, and in Australia for the Institute of Professional Editors.

See Appendix 1 for the editing exercise, "Critiquing a Passage."

# 16

# Common English and Style Errors

In Chapter 15, I mentioned that "standard" English actually varies considerably around the world. Still, some errors are the same, whether made in Australia, Britain, or the US. Here are 20 of the most common errors.

## Punctuation Mistakes

1. Comma splice (also known as the run-on sentence). A comma is not a strong enough punctuation mark to link two complete sentences, even if we think the sentences are closely related.

   *Incorrect:* She was Dad's senior clerk, her work was excellent.

   *Correct:* She was Dad's senior clerk; her work was excellent.

   *Correct:* She was Dad's senior clerk. Her work was excellent.

2. Misused semicolon. The semicolon can link two complete sentences that are closely related. It can't act to introduce an idea, like a colon, or link a phrase to a complete sentence.

*Incorrect:* Dear Mr. Smith;

*Correct:* Dear Mr. Smith:

*Correct:* Dear Mr. Smith,

*Correct:* Dear Mr. Smith

*Incorrect:* He was very happy; in fact, ecstatic.

*Correct:* He was very happy, in fact ecstatic.

3. Single comma between subject and verb. Some writers put in a comma just because that's where they'd draw breath if they were speaking the sentence aloud. Some also use it needlessly to set off a name from a title.

   *Incorrect:* The two persons who interviewed me, seemed impressed.

   *Correct:* The two persons who interviewed me seemed impressed.

   *Incorrect:* Nobel Prizewinning economist, Paul Krugman writes a blog for *The New York Times*.

   *Correct:* Nobel Prizewinning economist Paul Krugman writes a blog for *The New York Times*.

4. Missing question mark. Sometimes we just forget we've framed something as a question.

   *Incorrect:* Who would have thought that this shy immigrant girl would run one of the biggest ranches in Nevada.

   *Correct:* Who would have thought that this shy immigrant girl would run one of the biggest ranches in Nevada?

   However, we might drop the question mark when we frame a request as a question out of courtesy. For instance: Would you please let me know how much it would cost to acquire the rights to the photograph of my great-grandfather.

5. Needless apostrophe. The apostrophe marks contractions (isn't) and possessives (John's). But it doesn't usually mark a plural.

   *Incorrect:* His idea's are brilliant.

   *Correct:* His ideas are brilliant.

However, we do use the apostrophe for the plurals of individual letters and numerals. For example: In his diary, his 7's look like 9's and his p's look like b's.

6. Missing apostrophe. When you do need it, you really need it.

   *Incorrect:* Its good to see he hasnt changed.

   *Correct:* It's good to see he hasn't changed.

7. Misplaced apostrophe. Some plurals that don't end in s form possessives like singulars, and a plural possessive ending in s puts the apostrophe after the s.

   *Incorrect:* We went from the womens' gym to the Smith's house.

   *Correct:* We went from the women's gym to the Smiths' house.

8. Needless hyphen. Hyphens have many uses, but they don't link a verb and an object.

   *Incorrect:* Thank-you for your letter.

   *Correct:* Thank you for your letter.

   Note: The expression does take a hyphen when "thank you" is used as an adjective: *I sent a thank-you note to the person I had interviewed.*

9. Misplaced hyphen. A hyphen can break a word or phrase at the end of a line, but a hyphen never starts a line. When it breaks a word at the end of a line, it should be between syllables.

   *Incorrect:* I studied the day-to

   -day operations of the comp-

   any.

   *Correct:* I studied the day-to-

   day operations of the com-

   pany.

10. Misused colon. The colon signals a list, or an explanation of something you've just read. But it doesn't have a place between a verb and its object. You wouldn't write "I love: you." Nor should you write the following:

*Incorrect:* When he arrived, he called: John, Judy, and Bruce.

*Correct:* When he arrived, he called John, Judy, and Bruce.

# Grammar and Usage Mistakes

11. Sentence fragment. Your sentence is a fragment when it lacks a subject or a verb.

*Incorrect:* They sent me to the Inuvik office. A lucky break for me.

*Correct:* They sent me to the Inuvik office, a lucky break for me.

*Correct:* They sent me to the Inuvik office, which was a lucky break for me.

*Correct:* They sent me to the Inuvik office. This was a lucky break for me.

12. Missing capital letter. Proper names, including names of languages, take capital letters.

*Incorrect:* I always got top marks in english.

*Correct:* I always got top marks in English.

13. Needless capital letter. Ordinary nouns, like the names of the seasons, don't take capitals.

*Incorrect:* That Summer I worked in the Tourism Industry.

*Correct:* That summer I worked in the tourism industry.

14. Subject-verb disagreement. Singular subjects take singular verbs; plural and compound subjects take plural verbs.

*Incorrect:* Rain and hail was falling as we left.

*Correct:* Rain and hail were falling as we left.

15. Misuse of "myself." It's not a synonym for "I" or "me."

    *Incorrect:* Dave and myself are going out.

    *Correct:* Dave and I are going out.

16. Dangling and misplaced modifiers. These can be tricky, because they can "sound right" while actually modifying the wrong thing.

    *Incorrect:* While lecturing to the class, a fly buzzed around the teacher's head. (Means fly was lecturing).

    *Correct:* While the teacher lectured to the class, a fly buzzed around her head.

    *Incorrect:* No one died in the blast, which was blamed on a buildup of gas by one town official. (Means official got too gassy!)

    *Correct:* No one died in the blast, which one town official blamed on a buildup of gas.

17. Misuse of indefinite pronouns. Terms like "each," "either," and "everyone" are singular but can be mistakenly treated as plurals.

    *Incorrect:* Each of the managers were advised by memo.

    *Correct:* Each of the managers was advised by memo.

    *Incorrect:* Either of the two choices were acceptable.

    *Correct:* Either of the two choices was acceptable.

    *Incorrect:* Everyone got out their calculator.

    *Correct:* They all got out their calculators.

    *Correct:* Everyone got out his or her calculator.

    *Correct:* Everyone got out a calculator.

18. Misuse of adjective for adverb. Adjectives modify nouns. Adverbs modify verbs, adjectives, and other adverbs.

    *Incorrect:* I thought I had done real good on the quiz.

    *Correct:* I thought I had done really well on the quiz.

19. Wrong pronoun case. This mistake is easy to make in sentences with compound subjects or compound objects:

*Incorrect:* Me and Dave studied all night.

*Correct:* Dave and I studied all night.

*Incorrect:* The teacher graded Dave and I unfairly.

*Correct:* The teacher graded Dave and me unfairly.

20. Mistaken abbreviation.

*Incorrect:* ect.

*Correct:* etc.

*Incorrect:* ie.

*Correct:* i.e.

*Incorrect:* PHD

*Correct:* Ph.D.

*Incorrect:* eg.

*Correct:* e.g.

*Incorrect:* et. al.

*Correct:* et al.

# 17
# Manuscript Format

While you're working on your manuscript, it can be any format you find comfortable. But when you submit it to a publisher, it ought to look as inviting, clean, and professional as you can make it. You want to make sure it's as readable (and correctable) as possible; don't give the editor an excuse to reject you because the manuscript makes his or her eyes hurt, or because he or she can't even find room to insert spelling corrections.

Many publishers will be quite specific about the format they require for manuscripts. If your intended publisher is one of those, follow their instructions very closely. But if you're not sure where your manuscript will end up, the following guidelines should help you create an editor-friendly manuscript.

Ideally, you'll submit your manuscript in laser-printed form. If you can't afford that, then use an ink jet printer — when used with good bond paper, it's almost as good as laser. Plain black ink on white paper is best.

Consider your choice of font. Sans serif fonts are legible, but not necessarily as readable as serif — that is, you can recognize a word or phrase quickly, but reading page after page would be exhausting. A boldface font is even worse. Serif fonts are more readable, so you may want to focus on these for the body of your manuscript text.

Most editors seem to like 12 to 14-point text, which is highly readable in most fonts.

Paper should be standard 8.5" x 11", 20 lb. white bond. Give yourself a margin of at least an inch top and bottom, and an inch to an inch and a half on the sides.

Double-space your text. Do not put an extra double-space between paragraphs, unless you want a similar gap on the printed page to indicate a change of scene or passage of time. Indent each paragraph about half an inch.

If you are using a font with letters that take up variable amounts of space, a single space after a period is enough. If you are using a typewriter or a monospace font like Courier, two spaces are better. Either way, a single space should follow every comma, semicolon, and colon. Use an "em dash" — like that one. Some editors will put spaces on either side of the dash, while others will put no spaces. Two hyphens -- like this -- are an acceptable substitute. Underline text only if you cannot italicize it.

Do not use a right-justified margin in your manuscript! It may look tidy, but it creates gaps between words that make reading hard. Avoid hyphenations. Also avoid "widows and orphans" — that is, a paragraph that begins on the last line of a page, or a paragraph that ends on the first line the following page. Most word processors will kick such paragraphs onto the next page. This may create wide lower margins, but it's better than breaking a paragraph.

Be sure that each page displays a plain Arabic numeral in the upper right-hand or lower right-hand corner. Otherwise, don't bother with a header.

On the next page is a sample manuscript page from a book I published in the 1990s. Note that while most text is double-spaced, while extended quotations are single-spaced with wider margins.

# EXAMPLE 4: SAMPLE MANUSCRIPT PAGE

Chapter 7

Schools and Technology

Meeting Yana and Yevgeni

In the late 1980s I began to get involved with computer-based distance education. It was a slow and clumsy business (at least I was slow and clumsy), but it began to show me what the medium could do.

A professor at Simon Fraser University helped to get me and my article-writing students linked by computer with journalism students at the Bauman Technical Institute in Moscow. We sent our articles (and a lot of my course materials) to the USSR by modem. The Novosti press agency translated everything into Russian, and then translated the Russian students' work into English and fired it off to us.

The impact on my students and me was extraordinary. We were suddenly dealing with real people on the other side of the planet. Their articles were vivid glimpses of their own world, like this short piece called "How I Spent Last Tuesday," by a young woman named Yana Tikhonova:

> Today is Tuesday. My boyfriend Yevgeny is back from the hospital. He served in Afghanistan and was wounded there. I waited for him for two long years. And finally we are together. I wanted to forget about anything else in the world. No way. On that day I had an exam in computer technology and design.
>
> I thought I knew the subject fairly well. I am a good student but my emotional state ruined all my plans.

# 18

# Libel and Other Legal Pitfalls

It's possible to get into big legal trouble because of what you write. The law can vary remarkably from one country to another — and even inside the same country.

Consider this section a very general guide to securing yourself against the law, with links to online resources in several English-speaking countries. If you think you may run into trouble because of what you're saying in your manuscript, consult a lawyer before you publish.

Defamation is the unconsented and unprivileged publication of a *false and malicious* statement which tends to injure one's character, fame, or reputation.

Let's break that down: "Unconsented" means that someone didn't agree to have you say something defamatory about them. "Publication" means a third person has become aware of said defamation. If I send you a defamatory letter, and your secretary opens it and reads it, that's an unconsented publication. You can probably sue me.

However, if you open the letter yourself and then show it to your secretary, you have consented to its publication. Now I'm off the hook.

Defamation that is written or otherwise recorded (for example, on videotape) is **libel**. In Canada and the UK, truth is usually a complete defense in a defamation suit — in other words, if I make a defamatory statement that is also true, I cannot be sued. This does not always seem to be the case in the US. Whatever the local laws, the prospect of a court case to determine the truth often deters writers of potentially defamatory material.

Some false statements may be either absolutely or conditionally **privileged**; in this case, the person who makes them cannot be sued for defamation. **Privilege** is a legal right to communicate defamatory information in certain situations. **Absolute privilege** in Canada applies in Parliament, before Royal Commissions, in court and at coroners' inquests. So all persons who take part in judicial proceedings are absolutely privileged to make defamatory statements, in speech or writing. Letters between parties or lawyers relating to a controversy are also privileged. So as a witness I can repeat a false and malicious statement made by someone else, but I will not be liable to a charge of defamation.

However, defamatory statements made outside the proceeding are not entitled to absolute privilege. In Canada and Britain, a Member of Parliament can say anything at all on the floor of the House — including defamatory remarks. Those defamed have a useful answer: to invite the MP to repeat the remarks "outside the House." If the MP does, he or she can be sued for defamation. (One or two Canadian federal and provincial politicians have lost such lawsuits in recent years.)

**Conditional or qualified privilege** applies when it is in the interest of all concerned that fear of lawsuits should not hamper communication. For example, a previous employer may speak frankly about an employee's performance without fear of being sued, even if the employer makes mistaken comments. However, the employer must take reasonable care that the information sent is accurate and expressed without intentional deceit or malice.

Conditional privilege does not cover defamatory statements unrelated to the purpose of the particular privilege. For example, an employee's sexual behavior is not relevant to job qualifications, so an employer who refers to such behavior is not protected by privilege. The former employer may lose the privilege if the response uses such violent or abusive language that the real motive is evidence of malice or some other improper purpose.

Even so, many employers are now so afraid of being sued that they will offer nothing about an ex-employee beyond the dates that the employee began and ended employment.

**Fair comment** is a defense against defamation in certain cases where a writer may criticize a figure in public life in strong terms, without fear of reprisal. An editorial writer can therefore attack a political figure as an incompetent hypocrite, for example. Even if the charge is untrue, the political figure must accept it as part of normal political debate.

Similarly, the editorial writer must accept similar criticisms from readers who may write letters to the editor. And, having joined in public debate, the letter writers are also vulnerable to criticism under the principle of fair comment.

This happened to me when I was an education columnist for a Vancouver paper, and I had to take my lumps. (Journalists considered it poor form to respond in print to such attacks from readers.)

But if a reader had ever said: "Kilian doesn't know anything about education, and what's more, he gives his students A's if they pay him a hundred bucks," I would have gone to court in a second. Such a remark would have been a false and malicious attack on my professional integrity, not a fair comment on my quality as a writer.

Years ago I wrote a book about the state of education in British Columbia. Knowing I was discussing some prominent politicians and educators, I took my manuscript to a lawyer to ensure that I hadn't gone over the line. This was a wise decision.

While most of my criticisms fell under the category of fair comment on public figures, the lawyer did find some potentially defamatory assertions. As I recall, the assertions were usually unpleasant wisecracks about some person's personal character or professional conduct, rather than about their political behavior. I removed them at once, and had no legal trouble at all when the book appeared. Since then I have taken very great care not to make such wisecracks.

A Google search turned up several sites that discuss defamation in some detail. Surprisingly, American sources seem to be mostly in legal texts. They're available from Amazon.com, but most are extremely expensive.

Wikipedia: Defamation (http://en.wikipedia.org/wiki/Defamation). Never trust everything you read in Wikipedia, since anyone can contribute to it and the information may be incomplete or plain wrong. But, this should give a reasonable overview of the issue and the terms involved.

Inisiyatif.net: Defamation — Libel — Slander: www.inisiyatif.net/arsiv/web/filtre/Defamation_eng.asp.

A collection of online articles on various aspects of the subject in different countries.

### Australia

Australian Defamation Lawyers: www.australian-defamation-lawyers.com.au

Electronic Frontiers Australia — Defamation Laws & the Internet: www.efa.org.au/Issues/Censor/defamation.html

*The Journalist's Guide to Media Law*, by Mark Pearson. Google Books: http://books.google.com/books?id=FimrdH7OOpAC

### Canada

Defamation in Canadian Cyberspace: (www.angelfire.com/ca2/defamation/main.html)

Defamation, Media Privilege and the Charter: Cusson v. Quan and Grant v. Torstar Corp — Part 1: www.thecourt.ca/2009/04/23/defamation-charter-cusson-v-quan-and-grant-v-torstar-corp

Invasion of privacy can be a hazard for some writers, especially if they're writing about ordinary persons rather than public figures. But public figures deserve privacy as well, and may take you to court to defend it.

In general, you're on safe ground if you're sticking to publicly known information. This can include vital statistics like birth and marriage dates, legal proceedings, and so on.

But if you obtain information normally considered private, like a person's medical records, you're probably exposing yourself to a lawsuit. That applies also to information obtained by illegal means like hidden microphones or trespassing. You could even be in trouble if you publish false information about the person even if it isn't defamatory — for example, getting their place and date of birth wrong.

Again, consulting a lawyer, or a book on law, is preferable to taking my advice.

Another source worth exploring is the Electronic Frontier Foundation (www.eff.org), which has a strong focus on promoting freedom of speech online and defending personal privacy.

# PART 4: MARKETING

# 19

# Rules for Marketing Your Book

The late American science-fiction writer Robert A. Heinlein created five rules for writers. They apply as much to nonfiction writers as to novelists. Heinlein argued that anyone who followed all five rules would eventually get into print. In general, I think he was right.

1. **Writers write.** They don't sit around wishing they had time, or that inspiration would strike. They write.

2. **Writers finish what they write.** No matter how unpleasant the book-writing process may become, completing the manuscript is vital. (This is where writing an online journal, or writing letters to yourself, can be so helpful: you can identify problems and find solutions very quickly.)

3. **Writers never rewrite except to editorial order.** That is, they outline so thoroughly that they know what's coming next and they get it right the first time. I have reservations about this rule, mostly because constantly re-reading your manuscript as you

write will teach you about what you really want to say. But it's wise, as Heinlein suggests, to avoid endless revising. Wait for your editor's more objective suggestions.

4. **Writers put their work on the market.** Instead of making friends and family read the manuscript, they find potential publishers, or an agent, and send it off.

5. **Writers keep their work on the market until it sells.** This means developing a thick skin about rejections. A form letter from a publisher ("Not really for us at this time") can be demoralizing. But a serious writer will simply send the manuscript to the next publisher or agent, and keep at it until someone recognizes its value.

With Heinlein's fourth and fifth rules in mind, let's look at how to market your book.

## Book Proposals and Outlines

In some cases a nonfiction book just demands to be written, whether or not a market exists for it. In other cases, the book will never happen unless a publisher offers a contract for it.

In both cases, the author will probably have to pitch the book with a proposal and outline. This is not as daunting as you might think. If your subject excites you enough to make you want to write a book about it, your enthusiasm be evident in the proposal. Since the proposal usually includes an outline, the exercise will require you to think about the detailed content of your book.

As you start researching possible publishers, you'll find that some won't look at anything except proposals submitted through agents. We'll discuss how to find an agent later, but for now let's focus on the education publishers who are actively recruiting new authors: If you're a college or university instructor, you've doubtless talked with the sales reps of education publishers, and you know they don't just try to sell you a new course text. They often want to know if you're working on your own textbook. Few general publishers are as interested in new writers as the education houses are. That's because a successful textbook can sell huge numbers of books. So the publishers are willing to put some of their profits from the big sellers into "grubstaking" new authors. Most of those authors won't hit paydirt, but they may be willing to gamble on you. Even if you're not writing a textbook, the guidelines offered by education publishers can be extremely useful as you put your proposal together.

For example, Pearson Canada has detailed instructions for proposing a post-secondary textbook (http://www.pearsoned.ca/highered/main_content/proposal.html). The same page also lets you download detailed guidelines and even pitch your idea to an editor electronically, just to see if it stirs interest.

Other Pearson imprints around the world offer other guidelines based on their particular requirements and audiences. Skimming a few of these should give you a fuller idea of how you might pitch your book, and where.

One of the key elements in your proposal should be your assessment of the market and the possible competition for your book. If you show that you know what's going on in your field, and you see a missed opportunity that can be rectified with your book, publishers will treat your proposal with more respect.

Going online is a quick way to find out if someone else has already written your book. So if I were thinking of writing a history of North Vancouver, where I live, one place to start would be Google Books. I'd find a dozen hits for "North Vancouver history." Going to Amazon.ca (the Canadian branch of Amazon.com) would get me 18 hits.

Does this mean I should give up all hope of writing my history? Maybe, but not necessarily! Obviously these are books I should read, if I haven't done so already. I may find that they're dated, or narrowly focused on one aspect of the community. Some may have factual errors. Others may have missed some important archival resources that I have access to.

If I can find a special angle for my book, I may well be able to build a successful proposal around that angle.

Here's a little autobiography. In the 1990s, Self-Counsel Press approached me to see if I'd like to write a book in their series for writers. That turned into *Writing Science Fiction and Fantasy*, which went over very well. While it was in progress, and my editors were reading the early chapters, I pitched them with another idea — a book on writing for the Web. This was a brand-new subject back then, and Self-Counsel asked for a proposal. See Example 5 for what I sent them.

Looking back at this pitch after a decade, I can see how dated it looks (Globetrotter is a long-forgotten web application). The book that emerged from my proposal has done well, however, with a fourth edition published in 2009. Much of the content has changed. Despite this, the basic elements of my proposal are the ones you should consider integrating into your proposal:

- Problem: Something that's wrong with, or lacking in, the field that interests you.

- Solution: A book that deals with the problem in ways no other book has managed.

- Your qualifications: What makes you the person to write the book.

- The outline: What this book would deal with, in some detail.

Putting such a proposal together is at least as helpful for you as for your potential publishers. It makes you think hard, and in detail, about what's going to be in this book. Your publisher will be happy to see the thought you've put into it. When you get into the actual writing of the book, you'll be glad that you have a detailed outline to follow.

## EXAMPLE 5: Sample Proposal

Proposal for
*Writing for the Web*
by Crawford Kilian
[Postal Address]
[Phone Number]

**Premise:**

The curse and the glory of the World Wide Web is that no one understands it yet. As a communications medium, its impact is obvious, yet hard to define. Everyone comes to it with different habits and attitudes. CNN treats the Web like very slow TV. Newspapers treat the Web like a very clumsy newspaper. Businesses treat the Web like a very small billboard. And most people who write for the Web are more worried about the HTML, instead of what goes between the HTML.

Hundreds of books have appeared recently about designing Web pages, jazzing up pages with graphics and sounds and links. Scores of thousands of individuals and organizations are creating Web pages, with millions more likely to do the same within a few years—but no one has brought out a book on the real killer app for the Web: the English language.

The Web is a different medium from print, and demands a different kind of writing. It's also a different medium from TV, but our print and TV habits influence the way we respond to text on the computer monitor. Effective Web creation doesn't just mean cool video, graphics and sounds—it also means text that people will want to read, even if it means they stop surfing.

**Writing for the Web** offers some principles that writers can bear in mind, plus exercises to strengthen their writing skills and to sensitize them to their own bad habits. The principles derive not only from the author's experience, but from that of organizations that depend on computer-mediated communications for their very existence.

**Author's Qualifications:**

Crawford Kilian has taught clear, practical writing for 30 years. He's a Net veteran who's been teaching and writing online since the 1980s. He's taught computer students how to write interactively, both for multimedia and for the Web. He's taught online courses in writing, and served twice as a Writer in Electronic Residence with York University. His 18 books include **The Communications Book: Writing for the Workplace**, plus 11 science fiction and fantasy novels. His articles on computers' impact on discourse and education have appeared in such periodicals as *Internet World, Infobahn, Educom Review, Technos, Education Digest,* and the Toronto

*Globe & Mail.* (See the attached bibliography for details.) He's even beta-tested a new Web tool, Globetrotter (and loved it).

### Outline for *Writing for the Web*

**Introduction: The Nature of the Medium**

Monitors slow down reading speed, weaken proofreading ability.

Web users, not authors, determine appearance of pages.

On-screen text works better as caption than as detailed argument.

Computers, like TV, train us to expect frequent "jolts" from what we see and read, make us impatient with delay.

Graphics, sound can be "vampire video," "banshee audio," that undercut text.

Displaying text for maximum readability.

**Hype and Hypertext**

The myth of the author-oppressor in linear text.

Hazards for print-oriented writers and readers.

Visualizing your own hypertext.

Organizing hypertext: scroll versus stack, hit & run versus archive.

Building in navigational aids.

The chunk — basic unit of hypertext, a screenful of information.

Sequencing hypertext: anticipating reader response; lists; overviews.

**Writing Good Web Text**

Organize consciously: narrative, logical and categorical structure.

Activate the passive.

Prefer concrete Anglo-Saxon words to Greco-Latin abstractions (within limits).

Prefer common words to unusual ones.

Prefer simple sentences to complex ones.

Avoid clichés *like the plague* — especially web clichés.

Prefer strong verbs over weak ones.

Cut adjectives and adverbs.

Exercises for developing clear, short text.

**Editing Web Text:**

Trash your spellchecker — but check your readability level.

## EXAMPLE 5: Sample Proposal (Continued)

Cut verbiage.

Write out a critique of your text.

Print out to proofread — in an unfamiliar font.

Editing usage for international readers: advertise or advertize, labor or labour?

Common errors.

Editing exercises.

**Personal Pages, Résumés, and Self-Marketing:**

Getting beyond (but learning from) the print résumé.

Surprise: Redefining yourself as really different.

Getting the right nonverbal message across.

Providing useful services for your reader.

Making it easy for readers to respond.

**Advocacy and Marketing on the Web:**

Semantics and register: choosing the right words.

Basics of persuasion.

Avoiding propaganda techniques.

Logical argument on the Web: an oxymoron?

Social and political advocacy.

Marketing and sales promotion.

**Can You Write Fiction for the Web?**

Yes...sort of.

Self-publishing fiction on your website.

Hypertext fiction.

**Appendix: English Basics for Web Writers**

Concise information on grammar, spelling, punctuation, and usage.

Suggested reference works.

# 20

# Researching Publishers and Agents

Too many people submit manuscripts to publishers. Simply to read enough of each manuscript to judge it unworthy would take the full-time services of several salaried editors. Most publishers simply can't afford to pay editors to plow through the slush pile in hopes of some-day finding a Great Writer.

Some publishers indicate on their websites that they will consider only "agented submissions" — work that a professional literary agent who knows the market thinks has some sales potential.

That simply draws fire onto the agents, who now find that they too have huge slush piles. And, like the publishers, the agents can't make money reading junk they can't sell.

Where does that leave you? You're in better shape than you think. If you've hammered out a decent proposal and outline, you've maybe published an article or two, and you can write a grammatical sentence, you're already ahead of 80 percent of your competition.

Now the problem is finding the right market. Publishers tend to carve out special markets for themselves. A couple of sharp editors can dominate a genre; because they know how to reach a certain kind of reader, they attract a certain kind of writer. Or a publisher may be passionately devoted to supporting a certain kind of book, but is deeply uninterested in any other kind. And so on.

So step one is almost embarrassingly obvious: *Notice which houses publish the kind of book you're working on.* Out of all the publishers in North America, only a few are potentially interested in you.

Then consult those potential publishers' websites and see what they have to say about their own needs and who their editors are in specific nonfiction genres. You may learn that your work in progress is too long, or too short, or needs some particular quality. You may also learn how long it takes them to respond to queries and submissions. Don't take those statements as legally binding promises; responses almost always take far longer, especially for unagented submissions.

You may also want to consult resources like *Writer's Market*. This is a yearly publication that also lists publishers by the genres they publish. This list can lead you to publishers you're not familiar with, but don't just rush your manuscript off to some publisher in Podunk. Check out the entries of these houses also, and also track down some of their recent titles in your genre. If they strike you as dreadful garbage, avoid them. Better to stay unpublished than to be trapped with a bad publisher.

Another useful source of research information is the publishing trade press. *Quill and Quire* in Canada, and *Publisher's Weekly* in the US, are much more up-to-date than any annual can be. So if the top political editor in New York has just moved to a new publisher, or a publisher is starting a new line of adventure travel titles, you may adjust your marketing strategy accordingly. Magazines like *The Writer* and *Writer's Digest* supply similar market news.

If every possible publisher warns you off with "No unagented submissions," you then have to go through a similar process with literary agents. See the end of this section for the URLs for lists of agents.

You probably need an agent in the city where most of your publishers are. That, as a general rule, means New York City. You also need an agent who knows the market for your particular genre, so your work will go as promptly as possible to the most likely markets. (Some agents may submit a work in multiple copies to all potential publishers; this can really speed up the process.)

But also bear in mind that the phone and email can put almost anyone in close touch with the New York market, so an agent in Chicago or Los Angeles or Miami may be quite as effective as somebody in Manhattan — and may also be familiar with regional publishers.

Consider whether you want a big agent with scores or hundreds of clients, or a small outfit. The big agent may have clout but little stake in promoting you; the small agent may work hard for you, but lack access to some editors. Talk to published writers, if possible, about their experiences with agents; sometimes a sympathetic author can suggest a good one.

No agent, however good, can sell your work to an editor who doesn't want to buy it. What the agent offers the editor is a reasonably trustworthy opinion about the marketability of a particular manuscript. It's in the agent's interest to deal only in work with serious sales potential, and to get it quickly into the hands of its most likely buyers.

You may therefore have to query a number of agents before you find one who's willing to take you on. Here's where you may find a problem: Some agents won't look at your stuff unless you pay them to.

If you agree to the agent's terms and pay him or her to read your work, the reading may give you a very frank response. Sometimes you'll get a detailed critique that may devastate your ego but teach you just what you need to learn. In some cases the agent will waive the reading fee if he feels you're a commercial possibility and you're willing to sign on as one of his clients.

But bear this in mind: Such an agent is making much of his or her living by telling people they can't write. If the agent were really good, he or she would be out promoting clients' work. A freelance editor could probably give you equally good advice, and probably charge you less. You could receive comparable feedback at a lower cost.

Sometimes an agent will take you on but strongly suggest certain kinds of revisions, or even that you tackle a completely different kind of book. Listen carefully; you're getting advice from someone who knows the market and wants to share in your prosperity. At least one of my books greatly profited from the advice of an agent who thought my proposed ending was a disaster.

Your agreement with an agent may take the form of a detailed contract, or a simple agreement over the phone, or something in between. Be sure you understand and accept the terms your agent requires: Will he or she change 10 percent of what the agent makes you, or 15? Will he or she charge you for photocopying, postage, and phone bills? Does he or she have control over all your writing, or just your nonfiction?

Once you do have an agent, don't be a pest. When the agent has something to report, he or she will let you know. If you've got something to report, like the completion of the manuscript or an idea for the next book, let the agent know. Otherwise, stay off the phone and stick to your writing.

In some cases, of course, you may find you've sold a book on your own hook and then decide to go looking for an agent. Under these happy circumstances you should find it fairly easy to get an agent's interest. If the publisher's already offered you a contract (and you haven't signed yet), an agent may be willing to take you on and then bargain a better deal for you. But you'll probably do all right even if you negotiate that first contract on your own. Most publishers are honorable and decent people; sometimes their integrity is positively intimidating. Even if they weren't honorable, your first book is likely to make so little money that it wouldn't be worth it to screw you out of spare change.

# Places to Look for an Agent (and Further Advice)

- Adler & Robin Books FAQ on Literary Agents and Publishing: www.adlerbooks.com/mostask.html

- Agent Query (database): www.agentquery.com

- Association of Canadian Publishers — Literary Agents: www.publishers.ca/publishing-literary-agents.htm

- Australian Literary Agents Association:
  http://austlitagentsassoc.com.au/finding.html

- eBook Crossroads — Literary Agents:
  www.ebookcrossroads. com/agents.html

- Google Directory Literary Agents:
  www.google.com/Top/Business/Publishing_and_Printing/
  Publishing/Literary_Agents

- Guide to Literary Agents (website for book):
  www.guidetoliteraryagents.com

- Nonfiction Words of Wisdom from Agent Ted Weinstein:
  www.guidetoliteraryagents.com/blog/Nonfiction+Words+Of+
  Wisdom+From+Agent+Ted+Weinstein.aspx

- Preditors & Editors Agent & Attorney Listing (includes warnings
  about questionable agents):
  www.anotherealm.com/prededitors/peala.htm

- Publishers Global.com International Directory of Literary Agents:
  www.publishersglobal.com/directory/suppliers-by-service.
  asp?vendors-of=Literary+Agent

- Writers' Union of Canada: Literary Agents:
  www.writersunion.ca/gp_literaryagents.asp

# 21
## Reading Contracts

When you do finally receive a publisher's contract, you may feel your heart sink. It runs to several pages of single-spaced text, highly flavored with legalese and organized in a daunting sequence of numbered paragraphs and subparagraphs. I've known Ph.D.'s who have felt intimidated by their first contract.

Actually, you should worry more about what *isn't* in the contract. Most of your contract is standard "boilerplate" text that protects you as much as the publisher. It is often possible, even for a novice, to negotiate specific aspects of the contract.

Still, it helps to know what you're getting yourself into, so let us take a look at some of the key passages you're likely to find in your contract.

## Delivery of "Satisfactory Copy"

If you're selling your book on the strength of sample chapters and an outline, your publishers want assurance that you'll submit the full manuscript (often with a copy), at an agreed-upon length, by an agreed-upon date. If your full manuscript doesn't measure up, or arrives too late, your publishers have the right to demand return of any money you've received.

In practice they're usually much more flexible. They may bounce your manuscript back to you with a reminder that you don't get the rest of your advance until the manuscript is "satisfactory." The publisher (or more likely the editor) will tell you in exquisite detail what you still need to do to achieve "satisfactory" status.

Remember that to publishers and editors, your manuscript is work. It needs to be scheduled for design, typesetting, and art, not to mention inclusion in the fall or spring catalogue. Some publishers produce books as uniform in size as cupcakes. So if your manuscript is too short or too long, more work will have to go into expanding or cutting it.

A late manuscript also means you won't collect the balance of your advance until it's satisfactory, and missed deadlines may also cause delays in final publication: Like any assembly line, a book has to be scheduled day by day.

## Permission for Copyrighted Material

If you want to include the lyrics of a pop song in your book, or quote something as an epigraph, it's up to you to obtain the rights to such material, and to pay for them if necessary. If you leave it to the publisher, he or she might charge you; without permission, if the book doesn't work without such material, the deal would most likely be is off with your publisher and you would have to repay any advance you've received. Obviously, this is an extreme case; normally you just drop the lines from the song or poem, and carry on.

You may also need to obtain permission from copyright holders if you plan to quote more than just a snippet of text from them. In general, you can contact the rights editor of your source's publisher, or the copyright holder directly. Again, this may require payment.

## Grant of Rights

You are giving the publisher the right to make copies of what you've written. These copies may be in hardcover, softcover, audio recording, filmstrip, comic book, or whatever. You are also specifying in which parts of the world the publisher may sell such copies. For example, a sale to a British publisher may specifically exclude North America, leaving you free to sell North American rights separately.

You may also be giving the publisher rights to sell foreign translations, to print excerpts in other books or periodicals as a form of advertising, or to sell copies to book clubs. Normally such sales require your informed, written consent. The contract normally specifies how much you are to be paid for such specialized sales of rights.

## Proofreading and Author's Corrections

You agree that you will proofread the galleys or page proofs of your book and return the corrected pages promptly. If your corrections amount to actual revision of the original manuscript, and will require re-typesetting more than 10 percent of the book, the publisher will charge you for such costs. This can very easily destroy any income you might have earned from the book.

## Advances and Royalties

This spells out how much the publisher will pay you, and when. The most common agreement is payment of one-third of the advance on signing the contract; one-third on delivery of a satisfactory complete manuscript; and one-third on publication date. You may be able to negotiate half on signing and half on delivery; otherwise, you are in effect lending the publisher some of your advance until a publication date that may be over a year away.

Royalties are generally a percentage of the list price of the book. For hardcover books, the usual royalty is ten percent of list price. So a book retailing for $34.95 will earn its author $3.50 per copy. For mass-market paperbacks, royalty rates can range from four percent to eight percent, usually with a proviso that the rate will go up after sale of some huge number of copies — 150,000 seems to be a popular target. A paperback selling at $7.95, with an eight percent royalty, will therefore earn you about 64 cents. A "trade" paperback, intended for sale in regular bookstores rather than supermarkets and other mass outlets, will probably earn a comparable rate; the list price, however, will likely be higher and the number of copies sold will be lower.

Whatever the royalty rates, you're likely to get only half as much for sales to book clubs or overseas markets. (This is especially painful for Canadian authors with American publishers: sales in your own country, as "foreign" sales, earn only half the US royalty rate.)

You will also agree to split the take from certain kinds of licensing sales. For example, if your book is a hardback and some other house wants to bring out a paperback edition, you can normally expect a 50 percent share of what the paperback house pays. Sometimes a paperback house will license a hardback edition (in hopes of getting more critical attention for your book and hence selling more copies in paperback eventually); in such a case you should expect 75 percent of the deal.

If you can possibly avoid it, do *not* agree to give your publisher a share of any sale to movies or TV. A film or TV show based on your book will boost your publishers' sales quite nicely; they don't need a slice off the top of a deal that will surely pay you more than the publishers did. But if the book seems highly unlikely to interest Hollywood, you might offer a slice of film rights in exchange for a richer advance, with a proviso that an actual film or TV sale will also produce an additional chunk of money from the publishers.

The publishers will not normally charge for the production of versions of your book in Braille or other formats for the handicapped. So you will get no money from this source.

Your publishers should state in the contract that they will supply you with two royalty statements a year. Each will cover a six-month reporting period, and each should arrive about 90 days after the close of that period.

So a statement for January-June should reach you at the end of September. This will probably be a computer printout, and may be confusing. But it will indicate the number of copies shipped, the number returned unsold by booksellers, and the number presumably sold. The publisher will hold back on some of the royalty "against further returns." Whatever remains is the actual number on which the publisher owes you money.

Chances are that your advance will have consumed any potential royalties for the first reporting period, and perhaps for the second as well. Once you have "earned out" your advance, however, you should expect a check with each royalty statement.

It's a sad fact of modern life that many publishers don't give advances at all. They're struggling in a tough market, where many booksellers will order titles and then return them within a few weeks if they haven't sold. So publishers are often unclear themselves about how many copies they've really sold, and their cash-flow problems can be horrendous. An author who forgoes an advance at least can look forward to a more substantial check with that first royalty statement.

Do not sign a contract unless it explicitly promises you at least two royalty statements a year. Some publishers promise a statement only after the book has earned out its advance. This means you may go for years — or forever — without knowing what your sales have been.

## Author's Warranties and Indemnities

Here you are promising that this is indeed your work and that it isn't obscene, a breach of privacy, libelous, or otherwise illegal. If you do get into trouble, you agree to cooperate with the publisher's legal defense, and you agree to pay your share of the costs instead of asking the publisher, booksellers, or others to do so. If the publisher's lawyer thinks the manuscript poses legal problems, you agree to make the changes required to solve those problems — or to allow the publisher to do so.

You may find an insurance rider as part of your contract; this is intended to protect both you and the publishers from suffering total financial disaster if you get caught in a losing lawsuit.

## Copies to Author

You will get a certain number of free copies, and will pay a reduced rate for more copies. That means you will still pay for those copies, and you should.

## Option Clause

Pay attention to this one! This says you are giving the publishers right of first refusal on your next book (or at least your next book of this particular genre). The option clause means the publishers will give the next book a close, prompt reading. You should expect a response within 90 days, but some contracts specify 90 days after publication of your current book. That means you might have to wait for months, maybe over a year, until the publisher sees the initial reaction to your first book.

In practice, though, you probably will get a quicker response than that. If the publisher does make you an offer, you have the right to refuse it; you can then take your second book to any other publisher you like. However, you can't sell it to anyone else unless you get better terms for it than your original publisher offered.

You may well find yourself trapped as a result. If you need money in a hurry, you may feel you've got to accept a bad offer rather than spend months or years shopping your book around the market until you find a more generous publisher. And then, of course, your second contract will include an option clause for the *third* book...

Your best hope in this case is that sales of the first book will warrant a heftier advance on the second or third book. And if the publisher still won't cooperate, you can then go to another publisher with at least some respectable sales figures that show you deserve a better deal.

## Going out of Print

If the publishers let your book go out of print, you can make a formal request for it to be reprinted; if they don't want to, you can then demand that all rights revert to you. You are then free to sell the book to another publisher. (I have done this a couple of times. You don't make as much money on the resale, but at least the book stays out on the market longer.)

You will probably not make any money from "remaindered" copies that your publishers may sell to a book jobber at a deep discount. In some contracts, however, you may indeed receive some percentage of such sales. It's also possible to buy copies of your book at a similar low price.

## A Word of Advice

If at all possible, go over the contract with the editor or publisher, asking whatever questions arise. Then take your contract to an agent, lawyer, or professional writer. Chances are that it's perfectly okay. But even if you don't find something sneaky in the fine print, you'll have a clearer understanding of what you and your publisher have committed yourselves to. If something arises later on, like a problem over the option clause or the frequency of royalty statements, it won't come as a total shock.

# 22

# Is Self-Publishing Right For You?

Some writers decide that the whole process of finding an agent or publisher is just too much trouble. They would rather publish and market themselves. Sometimes it's the right decision.

A generation ago, however, self-publishing was the last resort of the desperate. So-called "vanity presses" would take anything and print it, for a price. The author would pay for everything: editing, design, cover art, even marketing (which usually consisted of sending out review copies to newspapers that would never review a vanity-press book).

In return, the author would get a certain number of copies, and could distribute them on consignment to bookstores, or sell them by mail order. Since vanity-press books had a deserved reputation for poor quality, they didn't sell in great numbers.

A corporate variation of the vanity press has been around for a long time. Some commercial publishers will bring out company histories, or biographies of prominent businesspersons, if the subject subsidizes the costs of publication. In such cases the client may even choose the author; the publisher provides design, editing, and marketing.

Such "subsidy publishing" can bring out very worthwhile titles, with excellent writing and well-researched content. The books make nice gifts to company clients, and may be donated to lot of public libraries as a form of indirect advertising. But no commercial publisher would be willing to cover the whole cost of such a book.

After all, publishing a book is an expensive proposition. You need to hire designers, editors, publicists, artists, and printers. The printed copies need to be stored in a lighted, heated warehouse, and shipped to customers by clerical staff. Publishers who don't bring out very commercial titles will not stay in business for long, unless they're getting some kind of subsidy.

# Print-on-Demand

Starting in the 1990s, however, a new form of vanity publishing emerged. It became possible to store a well-designed, typeset book as a computer file. This cost almost nothing. A "print on demand" (POD) publisher doesn't need a warehouse or all those expensive specialists on the payroll. If an order comes in for one copy, or a hundred copies, producing and shipping costs for that order are very inexpensive.

When the first POD publishers launched, they needed a "backlist" of titles, and one such publisher approached me. I had a number of out-of-print novels; would I give this publisher the right to print new copies?

I would and I did. Several of my novels are still available (with new covers), for very reasonable prices. I sent the publisher copies of those novels, which were scanned and stored electronically. The income from sales is very small, but it's better than no sales at all. My only real complaint is that the POD copies reflect the very bad scanning technology of the 1990s: The books are full of typos.

But POD has its pitfalls as well: Costs can be high, product quality can be uneven, and sales are likely to be few.

The best single source of advice that I know about POD publishing is Victoria Strauss's "Print on Demand Self-Publishing Services," on the website of the Science Fiction Writers of America (www.sfwa.org/ BEWARE/printondemand.html). While her emphasis is on fiction by new authors, her advice applies to nonfiction writers as well, and she provides plenty of links to other resources. While her view of POD publishing is generally negative, she does see some POD opportunities for nonfiction writers trying to serve a niche market.

## Serious Self-Publishing

Chances are that if you really wanted to publish books, you would have gone into the business. Many writers know they lack the time, talent, and interest to succeed in business in general, never mind the very tough business of publishing.

Still, some writers do have the business ability, or they're willing to acquire it. And they're also willing to invest their own money in their work. Like any business venture — even selling your own house — it may fail. But it sometimes succeeds very well.

Very roughly, the serious self-publisher will have to deal with a series of freelancers and small companies, probably including the following:

1. An editor (or editors) who can provide everything from substantive revisions to proofreading. (I recently saw a self-published book that was beautifully designed but embarrassingly full of the author's typos and spelling errors.)

2. A designer who can make the book look professional and attractive. Such a designer will almost certainly be proficient in an application like InDesign or QuarkXpress. The designer may also be able to create an effective jacket for the book. If not, you'll need to hire an artist.

4. A commercial printer who can give you an estimate on the costs of various options (number of pages, quality of paper, binding, and so on).

5. A lawyer to advise you on copyright and other issues, and an accountant to help you keep track of your publishing income and expenses.

6. A freelance publicist who can help promote your book.

7. A book-distribution company that can handle shipping. Otherwise, you're likely to have to drive around with a trunk full of copies, trying to charm booksellers into taking your book on consignment.

8. A web designer or hoster, if your self-made blog isn't up to the tasks of publicizing and selling copies of your book online.

And of course you'll have to interview and/or meet with several editors, designers, etc. before you settle on one.

Do some research before you commit to self-publishing. One good site is Publishing Basics (www.publishingbasics.com), which has plenty of hardheaded advice. It also offers a free downloadable e-book on what you should know, plus links to other useful sites. Use your online search skills to find other resources that could help your particular project.

Yes, this is all a lot of hard, expensive work. Is it worthwhile? For some self-publishers, very much so. Occasionally a self-published book does well, selling briskly in independent bookstores. (I don't know how often the big-box book chains pick up self-published titles.) Those sales figures may interest a commercial publisher in becoming your distributor. That gives you access to a much larger, more effective sales and distribution operation, and possibly even international sales.

It's often possible to use your self-published book in connection with conferences you attend and speeches you give. The book itself gives you credibility as an expert in your field, which means more invitations to be a keynote speaker or panelist at professional conferences. You can then sell copies to your audiences. (You may also want to make a deal with a speakers' bureau, which can publicize your availability and ask for fees that you would be embarrassed to demand.)

## Should It Be an E-book?

An e-book is certainly the easiest and cheapest way to publish. It can be as simple as making copies of your word-processed manuscript. More commonly, e-book authors turn their manuscript into a PDF file and send it off to anyone who asks for it. (You can even install a password on the PDF, so the reader has to pay you before getting access to it.)

Or you can design and typeset the book with InDesign or Quark-Xpress and make it available to purchasers — perhaps by printing off a copy each time a request comes in.

Again, online research can help you decide on this option. Here are some resources with which to start:

- Adobe Forums: Acrobat e-books:
  http://forums.adobe.com/community/acrobat/acrobat_ebooks

- GuidetoE-bookMarketing.com:
  www.guidetoebookmarketing.com

- Skelliewag: How to Create and Publish Your Own eBook with a $0 Budget:
  www.skelliewag.org/how-to-create-and-publish-your-own-ebook-with-a-0-budget-53.htm

- Suite101.com: Creating an E-Book in QuarkXpress:
  http://designingbooks.suite101.com/article.cfm/creating_an_ebook_in_quarkxpress

- Create a Website: Creating an e-book with Adobe Acrobat (video):
  http://blog.2createawebsite.com/2009/06/01/creating-an-e-book-with-adobe-acrobat/

With the advent of improved e-book readers like the Kindle, the market is likely to improve. For specialized topics (and books much shorter than the usual length of a book in print), an e-book may be your best solution. But you may also find, as a self-publisher, that you can produce both paper and electronic versions of your book, expanding your market.

# Is Writing Nonfiction Worth Doing at All?

Statistically, you're unlikely to make significant income from writing nonfiction books. The market is too uncertain, the return on invested time and energy too low.

Yes, an occasional textbook succeeds enormously, thanks to a captive student market. A celebrity confession, a political memoir, or a travel book may find huge and appreciative audiences. But most nonfiction books sell a few hundred to a few thousand copies, and vanish.

Look at Amazon.com's list of its top 25 sellers in nonfiction (www.amazon.com/gp/bestsellers/books/53/ref=pd_ts_b_nav). When I did so in mid-2009, eight of the top titles were advocating some form of American conservatism. Don't bother to drop your current project to bash out a new right-wing polemic — by the time you're ready to market it, something else will be the hot subject.

But your book offers you some other kinds of rewards. First of all, just writing it is great exercise. Good writing follows good thinking. That feeling of exhaustion and frustration when you're writing is exactly like the ache in your legs after a long run or workout in the gym: To find just the right words, in the right sequence, your brain demanded more of your body's resources than it usually does, and it probably had to grow some new neuronic connections as well. Every sentence you write leaves you in better mental shape.

Secondly, if the subject of your book interested you in the first place, writing in detail about it should have deepened and broadened your interest. Whether it's the real pirates of the Caribbean, or the siege of Vicksburg, or the life of your great-grandmother, you now know more about it, and you have done yourself a great favor.

Thirdly, you've taught yourself some highly transferable skills about finding, organizing, and presenting information on a particular topic. If the next thing you write is a memo to your boss, or a report on this year's county fair, it will be a good one. Your readers will wonder how the heck you learned all that, and how you made it all so clear and interesting.

Fourthly, if you've gone online to research, write and market your book, you're now far better equipped than most people to exploit this remarkable new medium. Even the teenagers who are supposed to be so internet-savvy barely understand what's out there.

In the two or three years before I retired from college teaching, I made a point of taking each of my classes into a computer lab. I showed them some of the search techniques in this book, and they were amazed and delighted — they'd always just clicked on "I feel lucky" and hoped for the best.

Mastering those search techniques is fun as well as practical, and it should help you to write your nonfiction book far faster than you could without them. Then you can go on to the next project, whatever it may be, and complete it faster as well.

You will find further support, online resources, and encouragement at my blog: http://crofsblogs.typepad/com/nonfiction.

I wish you every success.

# Appendix I:
## Editing Exercises

## Bafflegab

**Redundancy: Saying the Same Thing Twice**
The unneccessary words in each phrase can be removed.

~~horizontally~~ level             ~~actual~~ experience

read ~~through~~                   maximum ~~possible~~

~~physical~~ size                  hexagonal ~~in shape~~

~~final~~ outcome                  contains ~~within~~

**Superfluity: Using Needless Words**
Omit the unneeded words or rearrange phrases to promote clarity and simplicity.

numerals ~~are used to~~ identify

will not ~~properly~~ align

deal with theft ~~if and when it occurs~~

turn the dial ~~when required for adjustment~~

gasket ~~located~~ inside the device

~~in order~~ to compete with

## Pomposity: Twelve-Dollar Words for Two-Bit Ideas

Here are some synonyms to help make your phrase more readable.

| | |
|---|---|
| terminate: end | optimum: best |
| institute (verb): start | elevated: raised |
| initial: first | purchase: buy |
| expenditure: spending | facilitate: ease |
| demonstrate: show | operate: run |
| subsequent: later | expedite: hasten |
| prior to: before | investigate: study |
| excessive quantity: too much | adhere: stick |
| peruse: read | scrutinize: examine |

## Anemic Verbs: Action Words That Don't Do Anything

Provided are some alterations for unnecessarily lengthy phrases.

provides continuous indication of: continuously indicates

permits the reduction of: reduces

perform the measurement: measure

makes for improved employee morale: improves employee morale

by exerting a twisting action: by twisting

helps in the production of: helps produce

make the adjustment: adjust

functions to transmit: transmits

## Verbosity: Using Four Words When Fewer Would Do

Here are some ways to make your writing sound less technical.

caution must be observed: be careful

atmospheric moisture content: humidity

large number of: many

it is imperative that employees: employees must

the parts in some instances were defective: some parts were defective

takes into consideration: considers

is provided with: has

through the medium of radio broadcasts: by radio

for the reason that: because

in the event that: if

# Editing Exercise 1: Critiquing a Passage

Here is a 270-word passage that needs serious revision. After you read it, jot down your ideas for substantive editing, line editing, and copy editing. Then compare your comments with my critique following the passage.

Beginning in 1891 as a company town built by the Chesterton Logging Co., Chesterton grew to become a thriving community of over 3,000 men, women, and children. During World War I, the population grew still more to meet the demand for spruce to build airplanes, the population rose to almost 4,000. After the war, a zinc mine went into operation at the base of Mount Freeman (named for pioneer trapper Daniel Freeman, who conducted an exploration of the region in the 1820s). The conduct of mining operations paid off bigtime with great prosperity in the late 1920s, even after the Chesterton sawmill shut down. But then with the Great Depression the zinc market collapsed and hundreds of workers lost there jobs. Chesterton's population shrank to not much more then 300 souls. The town was at deaths door. After World War II, however, the creation of Chesterton regional park brought about a new rebirth for the town. As tourism began to grow, the community found a new lease on life catering to skiers, hikers, and campers. In the past 10 or 20 years, Chesterton has seen the development of world-class skiing at High Corniche, the North American Kayak Championships at Roaring Creek, and a booming whitewater rafting business that puts almost 200 rafts into the Old Horse River every Summer season. With 1,200 year-round resident, Chesterton is now a major recreation center and eco-tourism destination. Chesterton, after decades first as a logging town and Mining centre, and then as a seriously depressed community very nearly became a ghost town, is now making a comeback as a major tourist destination.

Compare your comments with my critique and revision below.

Substantive editing issues: We don't know where this passage is going when we start it, and we don't know why we should read it. The text is a single long paragraph, roughly in chronological order. The ending is repetitive.

Line editing issues: Tone and usage are inconsistent. "Paid off big-time" is too casual, and "at death's door" is clichéd. Is spelling Canadian or American?

Copy editing issues: Many spelling, capitalization, and punctuation errors.

A revised version of the passage:

Chesterton, after decades first as a logging and mining town, and after nearly becoming a ghost town, is now making a comeback as a major tourist destination.

Beginning in 1891 as a company town, Chesterton became a thriving community of over 3,000. During World War I, the population rose to almost 4,000 to meet the demand for spruce to build airplanes.

After the war, a zinc mine at the base of Mount Freeman brought great prosperity, even after the Chesterton sawmill shut down. But in the Great Depression the zinc market collapsed and hundreds of workers lost their jobs. Chesterton's population shrank to about 300.

After World War II, however, the creation of Chesterton Regional Park meant new hope for the town. As tourism began to grow, the community catered to skiers, hikers, and campers.

Chesterton has now seen the development of world-class skiing at High Corniche and the North American Kayak Championships at Roaring Creek. A booming whitewater-rafting industry puts almost 200 rafts into the Old Horse River every summer. With 1,200 year-round residents, Chesterton is now a major recreation center and eco-tourism destination. (Revised word count: 186)

# Editing Exercise 2: Editing Longer Passages

Here is an excerpt from *Go Do Some Great Thing: The Black Pioneers of British Columbia*. Go through it like an editor, cutting needless words, reorganizing text, and proofreading for typos and English errors. Then compare your version with the version following this passage.

Sometime in the mid-1860s, Wellington Moses arrived in the Cariboo. After wandering up and down the Fraser for a few years, he settled in Barkerville. Here he ran a sort of barbershop and dry-goods store, he offered everything from lady's shoes ("No more cold feet!" his ads promised) to his own reknowned Hair Invigorator, which he advertised in both the Cariboo and the Victoria papers:

"TO PREVENT BALDNESS, restore hair that has fallen off or become thin, and to cure effectually Scurf or Dandruff. It will also releive the Headache, and give the hair a darker and glossy color, and the free use of it will keep both the skin and hair in a healthy state. Ladies will find the Invigorator a great edition to toilet, both in consideration of the agreeable and delicate perfume, and the great facility it affords in dressing the hair. ... When used on childrens' heads, it lays the foundation for a good head of hair."

Although a single treatment cost $25 (about $320 in todays US dollars), he had a steady stream of customers for it, and some offered testimonials to its effectiveness in curing baldness.

Like most of the blacks in the gold country, Moses lead a quite, uneventful life. Most of his diary entries deal with the whether and his financial accounts, and little more. On one occassion, however, he helped to send a man to the gallows for murder.

In the Spring of 1866, Moses had travelled south to New Westminster, and on his return late in May he becomes the travelling companion of a young Bostonian named Charles Morgan Blessing. They left their steamer at Yale, the two men continued on foot toward

Barkerville, about 400 miles north. (A stagecoach had been in operation since 1864, but was probably to expensive for the barber and the
aspiring prospector.)

Blessing's appearance may have made him seem more prosperous then he was: he sported an unusual tiepin, with a gold nugget
naturally shaped like a man's profile.

At Quesnelmouth they encountered another man, James Barry,
who was also looking for company. Moses planned to break his journey for a few days, Blessing was impatient to go on. As Moses later
testafied, Blessing was a timid man, he distrusted most people, and
he had reservations about Barry. He was carrying fifty or sixty dollars
(about $650-$750 in todays money). Not a large sum, given the cost of
living in gold country, and he worried about being robbed.

Overcoming his fears, Blessing left with Barry after agreeing to
meet Moses at Van Winkle, a mining camp on the road to Barkerville.
When Moses reached Van Winkle, he found no sign of Blessing and
went on to Barkerville. A few days later he meets Barry in the street.

"What have you done with my chummy?" Moses asks.

"Who? Oh, that coon. [Since Blessing was white, it was an odd
term for him.] I have not seen him since the morning we left the Mouth.
I left him on the road. He could not travel; he had a sore foot."

Moses saw Barry twice more in following days, and each time
asked about Blessing; the third time, Barry "looked savagely" at him,
and muttered something under his breath.

One day in October, Moses was shaving a customer and noticed
the man's tiepin. It was obviously Blessings: a nugget with a man's
profile.

"Where did you get that?" Moses asked.

"From a hurdie," the man says. The hurdy-gurdy girls of the Cariboo dance halls where understandably popular in a country with few women. Moses in turn was popular with them, since he stocked ladie's clothing and perfume, and often lent the girls money. He soon found the hurdie, she told him James Barry had given her the pin some time ago.

Moses went to Judge Cox in nearby Richfield, now alarmed and suspicious. By coincidence, a report had just come about the discovery of Blessing's body, not far from where he and Barry had last been seen together. Blessing had been shot once, in the back of the head, and his body had been concealed in some dense bush some forty yards below the trail.

As soon as news of the murder became public, Barry dissappeared. On the strength of Moses's information, Judge Cox sent Constable John Sullivan out to track him down. Sullivan knew that Barry was surely heading south, he rode cross-country to try to intercept him at Soda Creek. He was to late, Barry had caught the stagecoach from Soda Creek to Yale.

Had he left a day or two earlier, Barry would almost surely of escaped, but as it happened the telegraph line from New Westminster had just been completed as far as Soda Creek. Sullivan sent the first message south, describing Barry to the authorities at Yale. When they took him off the stage, Barry gave a false name; undeceived, the local constable sent him back north.

As Sullivan took custody of the fugitive, Barry asked what he was charged with, and who had laid the charge. Sullivan replied that he would be told the details when they reached Richfield.

"It is the coloured man, Moses the barber," Barry said. 'He was always asking me what had become of a man who had come up with me, and at last I got vexed and told him, I was no caretaker of that man.'

Barry was jailed until the next assizes, in July 1867. Judge Begbie heard the case, including the testimony of Wellington Moses. He identified several personnel items that had been found on Blessing's body, including a knife, watch, and pencil case. He also recalled that before leaving with Barry, the young man had said to Moses: "My name is Charles Morgan Blessing. Be sure to recollect it if anything should happen to me in this country." He had also mentioned having $50 or $60 left. Other witnesses confirmed that Barry had been broke in Quesnelmouth but had been spending money in bars and on the hurdy-gurdy girls in Barkerville and Cameronton.

Though all the evidence was circumstantial; it was certainly enough to convict; the jury took only an hour to find Barry guilty. Next day, Begbie summoned the prisoner and asked if he had anything to say before sentence was passed. Barry began an incoherent story about leaving Blessing with a stranger while he himself went on with a party of Chinese. Then, like he knew it was futile, he said: "This is all the statement I want to make." As Begbie concluded in his report of the trial, "Sentence of death was then passed in the usual way."

Barry's death warrant, with its official seal pressed into black wax, was issued on July 16. Three weeks later he was hung at Richfield. Moses, meanwhile, had took up a collection to give Charles Morgan Blessing a proper funeral in Quesnel and to put a headstone and railing on the young man's grave.

That grave is now British Columbia's smallest provincial historic site. As well, a memorial plaque to Blessing stands at Kilometer 43 on Highway 26 between Quesnel and Barkerville.

Here is the text as it appeared in *The Tyee*:

Sometime in the mid-1860s, Wellington Moses arrived in the Cariboo. After wandering up and down the Fraser for a few years, he settled in Barkerville. Here he ran a sort of barbershop and dry-goods store, offering everything from ladies' shoes ("No more cold feet!" his ads promised) to his own renowned Hair Invigorator, which he advertised in both the Cariboo and the Victoria papers:

"TO PREVENT BALDNESS, restore hair that has fallen off or become thin, and to cure effectually Scurf or Dandruff. It will also relieve the Headache, and give the hair a darker and glossy color, and the free use of it will keep both the skin and hair in a healthy state. Ladies will find the Invigorator a great addition to toilet, both in consideration of the agreeable and delicate perfume, and the great facility it affords in dressing the hair. ... When used on children's heads, it lays the foundation for a good head of hair."

Although a single treatment cost $25 (about $320 in today's US dollars), he had a steady stream of customers for it, and some offered testimonials to its effectiveness in curing baldness.

Like most of the blacks in the gold country, Moses led a quiet, uneventful life. Most of his diary entries deal with the weather and his financial accounts, and little more. On one occasion, however, he helped to send a man to the gallows for murder.

In the spring of 1866, Moses had travelled south to New Westminster, and on his return late in May he became the travelling companion of a young Bostonian named Charles Morgan Blessing. Leaving their steamer at Yale, the two men continued on foot toward Barkerville, about 400 miles north. (A stagecoach had been in operation since 1864, but was probably too expensive for the barber and the aspiring prospector.)

At Quesnelmouth they encountered another man, James Barry, who was also looking for company. Moses planned to break his journey for a few days; Blessing, however, was impatient to go on. As Moses later testified, Blessing was a timid man who distrusted most people, and he had reservations about Barry. He was carrying fifty or sixty dollars (about $650-$750 in today's money) — not a large sum, given the cost of living in gold country, and he worried about being robbed.

Blessing's appearance may have made him seem more prosperous than he was: he sported an unusual tiepin, with a gold nugget naturally shaped like a man's profile.

Overcoming his fears, Blessing left with Barry after agreeing to meet Moses at Van Winkle, a mining camp on the road to Barkerville. When Moses reached Van Winkle, he found no sign of Blessing and went on to Barkerville. A few days later he met Barry in the street.

"What have you done with my chummy?" Moses asked.

"Who? Oh, that coon. [Since Blessing was white, it was an odd term for him.] I have not seen him since the morning we left the Mouth. I left him on the road. He could not travel; he had a sore foot."

Moses saw Barry twice more in following days, and each time asked about Blessing; the third time, Barry "looked savagely" at him, and muttered something under his breath.

One day in October, Moses was shaving a customer and noticed the man's tiepin. It was obviously Blessing's: a nugget with a man's profile.

"Where did you get that?" Moses asked.

"From a hurdie," the man replied. The hurdy-gurdy girls of the Cariboo dance halls were understandably popular in a country with few women. Moses in turn was popular with them, since he stocked ladies' clothing and perfume, and often lent the girls money. He soon found the hurdie, who told him James Barry had given her the pin some time ago.

Now alarmed and suspicious, Moses went to Judge Cox in nearby Richfield. By coincidence, a report had just come about the discovery of Blessing's body, not far from where he and Barry had last been seen together. Blessing had been shot once, in the back of the head, and his body had been concealed in some dense bush some forty yards below the trail.

As soon as news of the murder became public, Barry disappeared. On the strength of Moses's information, Judge Cox sent Constable John Sullivan out to track him down. Sullivan knew that Barry was surely heading south, and rode cross-country to try to intercept him at Soda Creek. He was too late: Barry had caught the stagecoach from Soda Creek to Yale.

Had he left a day or two earlier, Barry would almost surely have escaped, but as it happened the telegraph line from New Westminster had just been completed as far as Soda Creek. Sullivan sent the first message south, describing Barry to the authorities at Yale. When they took him off the stage, Barry gave a false name; undeceived, the local constable sent him back north.

As Sullivan took custody of the fugitive, Barry asked what he was charged with, and who had laid the charge. Sullivan replied that he would be told the details when they reached Richfield.

"It is the coloured man, Moses the barber," Barry said. "He was always asking me what had become of a man who had come up with me, and at last I got vexed and told him, I was no caretaker of that man."

Barry was jailed until the next assizes, in July 1867. Judge Begbie heard the case, including the testimony of Wellington Moses. He identified several personal items that had been found on Blessing's body, including a knife, watch, and pencil case. He also recalled that before leaving with Barry, the young man had said to Moses: "My name is Charles Morgan Blessing. Be sure to recollect it if anything should happen to me in this country." He had also mentioned having $50 or $60 left.

Other witnesses confirmed that Barry had been broke in Quesnelmouth but had been spending money in bars and on the hurdy-gurdy girls in Barkerville and Cameronton.

Though all the evidence was circumstantial, it was certainly enough to convict; the jury took only an hour to find Barry guilty. Next day, Begbie summoned the prisoner and asked if he had anything to say before sentence was passed. Barry began an incoherent story about leaving Blessing with a stranger while he himself went on with a party of Chinese. Then, as if realizing it was futile, he said: "This is all the statement I want to make." As Begbie concluded in his report of the trial, "Sentence of death was then passed in the usual way."

Barry's death warrant, with its official seal pressed into black wax, was issued on July 16. Three weeks later he was hanged at Richfield. Moses, meanwhile, had taken up a collection to give Charles Morgan Blessing a proper funeral in Quesnel and to put a headstone and railing on the young man's grave.

That grave is now British Columbia's smallest provincial historic site. As well, a memorial plaque to Blessing stands at Kilometer 43 on Highway 26 between Quesnel and Barkerville.

# Appendix 2:

## Checklist for Nonfiction Writers

As you begin to develop the actual text of your book, you can save time and energy by making sure that your writing style requires virtually no copyediting.

1. Do any sentences begin with the words "There" or "It"? They will almost certainly benefit from revision. (Compare: There were three principles that guided his life. Three principles guided his life.)

2. Are you using passive voice instead of active voice? (Compare: Is passive voice being used?) Put it in active voice!

3. Are you repeating what you've already told your readers? Are you telegraphing your punches?

4. Are you using trite phrases, clichés, or deliberately unusual words? You'd better have a very good reason for doing so, like quoting a source word for word.

5. Are you terse? Or, alternatively, are you expressing your thoughts with a perhaps excessive plethora of gratuitous and surplus verbiage, whose predictably foreseeable consequences, needless to say, include a somewhat repetitious redundancy?

6. Is grammar correct? Are spelling and punctuation correct?

7. Is the prose fluent, varied in rhythm, and suitable in tone to the type of story you're telling?

8. Are you as narrator intruding on the story through witticisms, editorializing, or self-consciously "fine" writing?

9. Where you are clearly citing one of your sources, is the citation clear, whether through footnoting or context?

10. Are you testing the readability of your text, and keeping the readability level as low as possible?